To Meg

Thank you for
buying my
book. Don't
forget to Feel
Yourself!
Love Nat x

Feeling Myself

Feeling Myself

Myself

HOW I SHED MY SHAME
TO FIND SEXUAL FREEDOM
AND YOU CAN TOO

Natalie Lee

Vermilion
LONDON

1

Vermilion, an imprint of Ebury Publishing,
20 Vauxhall Bridge Road,
London SW1V 2SA

Vermilion is part of the Penguin Random House group of companies
whose addresses can be found at global.penguinrandomhouse.com

First published in the UK by Vermilion in 2022

www.penguin.co.uk

A CIP catalogue record for this book is available from
the British Library

ISBN 9781785043864

Typeset in 11/16.6 pt Palatino nova Pro by Jouve UK, Milton Keynes
Printed and bound in Great Britain by Clays Ltd, Elcograf S.p.A.

The authorised representative in the EEA is Penguin Random House
Ireland, Morrison Chambers, 32 Nassau Street, Dublin D02 YH68

Penguin Random House is committed to a
sustainable future for our business, our readers
and our planet. This book is made from Forest
Stewardship Council® certified paper.

There's no need to keep searching any more.

You are safe and you are home.

Breathe – fully. And let your body feel at ease.

Contents

Introduction

I'm lying on the floor in a small room in north London, made comfortable with cushions and a basic white sheet. I had planned to come here for weeks, and before I arrived, I was nervous; I didn't know what to expect. Now, I'm completely naked, and a woman who I've just met is sitting between my legs with her index finger inside my vagina. I feel strangely peaceful, nourished and cared for. In fact, for the first time while doing something so intimate, I feel completely safe. I even briefly fall asleep with the stranger's finger still inside me. When I wake, I have newfound clarity. This, I realise, is a pivotal moment in my sexual evolution.

You may be wondering what the fuck I am doing. I don't blame you – I would have thought the same thing a few years ago. But I have come on quite a journey to reach this place. A place of healing and sexual freedom. Though, before we skip to the finishing line, you should probably know a bit more about the uphill battle it took to get here.

For much of my life, sex and shame have walked hand-in-hand. Growing up, there was a shroud of secrecy around sex; the adults in my life spoke about it only in hushed tones, so I absorbed the idea that it was dirty and needed to be hidden. Sex education at my school was simplified at best and sexist at worst: I learned that the purpose of sex was to get pregnant, and to pleasure a male partner. Enjoying sex, and giving it away freely, was something only 'bad girls' did; the kind of women who were desperate, morally questionable and would probably never find a husband. Inevitably, all these formative lessons shaped my understandings of what sex could and should be.

So, I felt shame about having sex in the first place, and what that might mean for my sense of 'goodness'. I felt shame about sexual experiences that happened to me without my consent, and I blamed myself for my role in them. I felt shame about enjoying pornography. I felt shame about finding it hard to reach orgasm, and shame about wanting to orgasm at all. I felt shame for my fantasies and desires that broke the mould of what I thought I should want. I was deeply ashamed of what my body looked like, and don't even get me started on how shameful I believed it was to touch myself. Sex and shame became so intertwined that I didn't even know it was possible to separate them.

Perhaps you have felt this too. Maybe you have been ashamed of what your vulva or nipples look like. Maybe you have felt guilty for mourning your lack of sex after childbirth. Maybe you have internalised shame for fantasising about a woman while having sex with a man. Maybe you have felt embarrassed about wanting sex too much, or for not wanting sex enough. If shame has infiltrated your sexual life in any way, shape or form, then this is the book for you.

Introduction

According to psychotherapist Charlotte Fox Weber, co-founder of therapists' collective Examined Life and author of upcoming book *What We Want*, shame is 'a sense of deep humiliation and a feeling of being intolerable, unacceptable, disgraceful. Whereas guilt says you *did* something wrong, shame says you *are* something wrong.'

These feelings can come from lots of different places, says Charlotte, but they mostly come from our social environment. They come from being told that we shouldn't do certain things; that we can't want certain things. They come from having feelings and experiences that sit outside of what we believe is our designated role in society. And unfortunately, when it comes to women and sex, our needs and wants have been suppressed for far too long.

Throughout centuries, women's role in Western society has been to make babies, raise children and remain obedient to men. We were taught not to rock the boat, not to step outside these parameters created for us. When religious structures reigned supreme, marriage was held up as a sanctity and women were expected to remain 'pure' for their husbands. Being sexual outside of marriage was the ultimate sin: your reputation would be tarnished forever, which would lead you into financial ruin and probably even death. Sex was simply a means to an end – social security and raising the next generation. It will shock no one to learn that these same rules didn't really apply to men, who have always been given a free pass when it comes to shagging. For years, society has sent the clear message that sex geared towards female pleasure is bad. Sex, unless in the 'safe' confines of marriage and

3

reproduction, is not something 'good girls' do. If you want to get ahead in life, you'd better keep your desires hidden and your labia tucked firmly away.

I know this all sounds like the stuff of a Shakespeare play or a Dickens novel. Of course, we do live in a much more permissive, open society now – and women are no longer confined to such strict roles. But this mentality has trickled down through generations. Deep-held beliefs don't disappear that easily, no matter how hard we try. And we can't ignore the fact that these mindsets remain as strong as ever in many parts of the world. In some countries, Female Genital Mutilation (FGM) is an ongoing practice, which can involve women having the external part of their clitoris (the most sensitive sexual organ on a female body) removed.

Not only is this a disgusting way of denying women pleasure, it's incredibly dangerous, and thousands of women die from the practice every year. Elsewhere, 'honour killings' (otherwise known as 'shame killings') are common practice, where women can be murdered for deviating from social norms, whether that's having sex outside of marriage or being a lesbian. It's deeply shocking – but even in the most progressive societies (like where I am in the UK), we're still infected with misogynistic, patriarchal ideas that police women's freedom and desires. It can be more insidious, like in the ways we insinuate a successful woman 'slept her way to the top', and the way the media treats women who have had multiple relationships, from Taylor Swift to Meghan Markle. You can deny it all you want, but I think there's still an underlying expectation that women should be pure, good and clean. We're supposed to keep everyone happy and deny any focus on ourselves. Enjoying sex – the ultimate primal, pleasure-driven act – seems incompatible with womanhood.

It's unsurprising, then, that so many of us have gone through life with warped ideas about sex. We've been led to believe that sex is just something we have to 'do' in order to pleasure a partner, and that men should be front and centre of any sexual experience. We've been taught that sex is transactional and characterised by power imbalances. As a result, so many of us have gone through our sexual lives having un-explorative or routine sex just because we think we should – rather than what actually makes us feel good. And far, far too many of us have spent our lives battling hatred for our bodies, suppressing shame that we aren't the 'right' kind of woman, having sex in the 'right' kind of way. I know I experienced all this. I was unable to understand, embrace and explore the full extent of my sexual being. I didn't know I was allowed to. Now, though, I know I'm not only allowed, but entitled to that. And I hope this book will act as your permission slip, so you can free yourself from the shackles of shame and embrace the beautiful, sexual being you were always destined to be.

If you follow me on social media, under the guise of Style Me Sunday, you might already know that I talk freely about body confidence, sex positivity and healing. My social media is a space of complete vulnerability, honesty and giving the middle finger to the parts of life that don't serve us. I don't hold back when it comes to exposing myself (physically and emotionally) and this book will be no exception. I'm more than willing to lay myself bare.

Feeling Myself

When we talk about sex, our conversations about it often feel sanitised and surface-level. We end up talking *around* sex, not really about it. But I want to do some *real* talk. Let's get into the topics that really mean something in our sexual lives: trauma; masturbation; faking it; motherhood – the lot. I've noticed in the past few years that we've begun to open up about sex (TV shows like *I May Destroy You* and *Sex Education* are partly to thank for that) but I still think there's a reticence to really *go* there, to tell the truth about our experiences.

That's why I wanted to write this book. It's a memoir about the role sex has played in my life, and how I've managed to gradually shed its partner-in-crime – shame – along the way. Each chapter will cover a different element of my journey, from a traumatic event that happened on an idyllic beach as a child, to my first confusing and disappointing sexual experiences with older men, to my better-late-than-never adventures in wanking, right through to having children, getting married, getting divorced, and discovering – on the floor of a toilet cubicle – new sides to my sexuality that I didn't know existed. Though this is first and foremost my personal story, I want you to discover a deeper understanding of your sexual self, too – so I've included information, expert advice and comments from friends where I think they might be useful. By being as truthful as possible, and not sugar-coating difficult topics, I hope my story will make you feel seen, heard and, hopefully, as you flick through its pages, you'll notice any feelings of shame falling away. (A big hope, I know, but I'm nothing if not optimistic).

Introduction

This book has been a long time coming. I have visualised it for many years, but I haven't been able to write it until now. I had to dig really deep and confront a lot of wounds in order to get the words out. It contains details of sexual trauma, heartbreak, and is a peek through the window to the darkest depths of my soul. It's amusing and titillating (I hope) in parts, but deeply painful in others. Please do handle it gently and lightly, especially if you have sensitivities around these topics. I would especially recommend treading with caution around the first chapter (trauma) as this contains details of sexual assault, and chapter two (virginity) could be uncomfortable reading too, as I describe a sexual relationship I had when I was only 13 years old.

I also want to mention that I use the words 'woman' and 'women' throughout this book when talking about my personal experiences because this is how I define myself, and also when I talk about the historical role of biological females in society. I know that not everyone identifies with the sex they were assigned at birth, and I know that this has a unique set of challenges when it comes to sex and shame. In fact, I'm certain that anyone who sits outside society's ideal of cis, white, heterosexual and male experiences some level of shame when it comes to sex. Although I can't speak about this from a place of experience, I hope that if you don't fit neatly into gender and sexuality binaries, you will still feel welcome here.

When I had that conversation with psychotherapist Charlotte Fox Weber about shame, she said something that stuck with me. 'The most dangerous thing about shame is how it insists on silence,' she said. 'It tells us to shut up, which is actually what makes it worse. The best thing we can do is drag shame into the daylight. Whatever it is we are horrified by, we can handle it better if we see it in the light of day. Things are scarier in the dark, and this is especially true of shame.'

So that's exactly what I want to do with the book – drag a life of sexual shame into the daylight. I hope that my story resonates with you, in one way or another. Perhaps, like mine, your first time having sex was a massive let-down. Maybe you spent your twenties chasing orgasms that just didn't seem possible. Perhaps you felt like you lost your sexual self after having children, and felt guilty for wanting more. Maybe you have just split up from a long-term partner, and you're nervous about putting yourself out there all over again. I want you to know that I am with you. We're in this together. We all have our own unique, beautiful stories, but we are connected in immeasurable ways.

Most of all, I hope that by sharing my own experiences of sexual shame, I might help you to release your own. After all, the only way we can truly break the silence of shame is to use our voices – and I'm about to raise mine.

1

Trauma

Sitting in a chair opposite my therapist, I finally decided to tell her the secret I had carried my whole life. My body felt like it didn't belong to me – my hands were sweaty and I felt a deep foreboding, like an inert rock in the pit of my stomach. I was 35, but I'd never spoken about what I'd witnessed sober before. Had my mind inflated the incident out of proportion? Had I made it up altogether? Was it reality, or did I just want sympathy? I took a deep breath, and began to describe what had happened.

I was four years old. My mum had taken me on a trip to the Caribbean to stay with my dad's family. Despite her rocky relationship with my father – who she wasn't with at the time – Mum believed it was important for me to stay connected to the other side of my family, especially being a mixed-race child. I was very little, so my memories are hazy, but I remember the culture shock of staying with a Caribbean family for the first time, like when I watched my grandfather cut the head off a live chicken in his backyard.

Mostly, though, I remember the warm sun on my skin, and the gentle swaying of palm trees.

On one particular day, Mum decided to take me to the beach by herself. She needed a bit of space, I think. Staying with family, especially when they're not your own, can be a bit (ahem) challenging. It was probably the most idyllic beach you've ever seen – the kind with bright white sand that feels like you're walking on a soft sponge, and sparkling turquoise waters glittering in the sunlight. It was completely deserted, which only added to the beauty. As we splashed around in the water, we marvelled at the tiny little fish circling our feet. After a while, Mum headed back to the beach to sunbathe, and I, not ever wanting to be too far away from her, followed her to play in the sand next to her, collecting pretty shells.

My hands started shaking as I began to recollect the next part. Out of nowhere, a man appeared and started chatting to Mum. He was from the local area and seemed friendly; he told Mum about the best beaches nearby, and she asked him for recommendations. I'm not sure how long they were speaking for, or the exact conversation that led to what happened next, but suddenly we were in the mangroves together, and Mum was screaming as he put his whole body on top of hers. I don't remember all the details; I can't picture what he looked like, or how long we were there for, because I have spent most of my life trying to forget. I tried to make myself believe that it didn't really happen. Yet, when I close my eyes, I can still hear the screaming and crying, and the anger in his voice. I tried to pretend it was a made-up story, part of my overactive imagination. But it did happen.

Trauma

The man raped my mum, in front of me, while I sat visibly distressed and confused on the sand next to her. Next to them. I can't have known exactly what was happening at the time, but I could sense my mother's fear and pain. I must've known that he was doing one of the worst things a human could do. When he was finished, he got up and said, 'If you say anything to anyone, I will find you and kill you.' He then disappeared into the bush behind us. That picture-perfect beach would reappear in my nightmares for many years to come.

What happened next is increasingly blurry, but my mum recently told me she grabbed me as soon as he was gone, and tried to find a way out. She was traumatised, in shock and disorientated and couldn't work out where we were, or how to get away. Eventually, we found a road and hailed down the next passing car, who happened to be a lone male. We had no choice; we had to get in. Thankfully he took us to the police station. I remember Mum being exasperated that not much was being done. I don't think they ever found the man who did that to her. To be honest, I don't think they cared much. I try not to think about what happened to him; how many other women he hurt, how much more trauma he caused. Mum got an early flight back to the UK on her birthday – she told me it was the best birthday present she ever got. She tried her best to shield me from the trauma we had experienced, and because I was so young, she desperately hoped I would forget what had happened. I think it was a coping mechanism; another layer of trauma thinking about how this incident would affect her daughter was probably too much for her to bear. We hardly ever mentioned it again.

When I told my therapist all this, tears appeared in her eyes, but I was emotionless. I felt like an observer hovering over the situation, seeing it unfold from above. My therapist would later tell me that this is normal – that our brains disconnect us from the traumatic events we experience, as a defence mechanism. She told me that my mum had been groomed; lulled into a false sense of security by a man who seemed genuine and kind. He betrayed both of us. When I thought about that little girl, I couldn't connect with her. I didn't know who she was. I didn't feel sad or sorry for her. In some ways, I felt guilty that I couldn't protect my mum. Even though I was only four, the guilt stuck like super-strong glue.

That single, terrifying episode had an earthquake-like impact that has reverberated throughout my life. It was the starting block for everything that came afterwards. My introduction to sex was abrupt and violent. Maybe your sexual journey started in a torturous way too. Thankfully, most people don't have these experiences from such a tender age, but, even so, trauma is an element of many women's sexual stories that we don't recognise as much as we should. Traumatic events trickle into all our lives in some way, and especially into how we approach sex.

*

I was born in west London in 1980. Maggie Thatcher was ruling with an iron fist, the economy was in turmoil, and there were near-constant strikes by the trade unions. My parents were barely out of their teens when they both ended up working at the same nightclub in London, trying to get by despite the raised duties on petrol, alcohol and tobacco. They had a whirlwind romance and fell in love hard and fast, and my mum quickly became pregnant. I don't think either of them were ready to be parents. My father certainly wasn't.

Mum came from a rigid Irish Catholic family, with a strict and firm-handed father who had served in the British Army, and a quiet, timid mother. They had settled in a seaside town and Mum was her parents' only living daughter; her disabled older sister had died at the age of seven, before Mum was born, and she had two older brothers. Based on the pictures I have seen, my mum was a beautiful bouncing baby with big dark hair and huge piercing blue eyes – she was the apple of her father's eye. But their relationship took a turn when she entered her teens and rebelled. She was often referred to as the black sheep in her family, and she ran away aged 17 to work as a secretary in London, posing for glamour magazines in order to make some extra money. Having a baby with a Black man was the icing on the cake for her already disappointed family, who were products of a still very intolerant and racist society. Other than secret letters with her mother, she had no contact with them for the next ten years. So there was a cloud of shame over me before I even reached the birth canal. And this shame has been a theme for me for much of my life.

My early years were tumultuous – not just because of that horrifying incident when I was four. I spent my toddler years in a council flat in Ladbroke Grove, on the 12th floor of the now-iconic Trellick Tower. The flats there now cost upwards of £700,000, but back then, the lifts stank of piss and people would take their lives by jumping off the tower on a fairly regular basis. Sometimes, I wonder whether those lifts still have the same stale scent of beer-infused urine. I don't think it was exactly the kind of place my mother wanted to bring up her first-born child.

My parents' relationship was also not doing well. They argued a lot. Mum has never said what went on in those early days of my life, but it must have been bad enough for her to run away in the middle of the night from the man she thought was the love of her life, with a three-year-old – me – in tow. She went on to have a relationship with an abusive man who sold cocaine for a living and stalked her for years after they finally split. She told me she reported him several times to the police but they weren't interested. His harassment only ceased when Mum saw his picture in the *Sun* next to a story that described his sentencing to eight years in prison for rape and blackmail.

Mum often recalls how she couldn't afford a cot, so she used a drawer instead. It did a perfectly good job, she said, until my feet reached one end and my head the other. At one point, while we were in temporary accommodation, she said she came close to giving me up to social services, because she was so desperate for me to escape these dire surroundings. There is so much more to this story, but that's not my story to tell.

I cannot imagine how awful it was for her, a young mother living in a new city, isolated from her family, with no support, in an incredibly volatile situation. As a mother now, I cannot even contemplate the utter despair and desperation she experienced. She must have felt so lonely and hopeless. I've since understood that manipulative men target women like my mum, who are vulnerable and in need of validation and protection. Time and again, she was a victim to the cruelty of men; a cruelty that was – and often still is – societally approved. She came of age in a time where men could be controlling and abusive, and suffer no consequences whatsoever. If we think it's bad now, it was even worse then. I have so much admiration for my mum, for making it through all of these awful experiences; for surviving, and eventually thriving.

After those rocky early years, our lives did eventually settle down. Mum moved to Wembley, where we stayed for the next 12 years, and she would go on to achieve a monumental amount, including a first-class degree from university while raising three children (my half-sisters, twins born when I was 14 years old). We were incredibly close (especially when there were no awful men around), and it often felt like it was us against the world. But Mum didn't show her love through displays of affection, kisses and cuddles, and sometimes she could come across as very cold, which I have struggled with for many years, especially since having my own children. I have since been able to understand that she showed her love in other ways. She made sure we always had a roof over our heads and materially I never remember wanting for anything as a child. That is huge considering she was a single parent of a mixed-race child in the eighties/nineties with little to no support. She made many sacrifices to make that happen – many of which I will probably never fully know, but I have an inkling that they were momentous, painful and very brave.

I would only see my dad intermittently throughout my childhood. I would frequently cry myself to sleep at night, questioning why my dad didn't want to be around me; why he didn't go out of his way to see me. I wondered what I had done to make myself so unlovable and undeserving of his affection. I dreamed about the conversations I would have when I next saw him; I'd be brave and tell him exactly how his lack of presence affected me. How every birthday was tinged with sadness when no card or phone call materialised. But when I did see him, I'd just be so happy to be in his presence for once that I wouldn't allow anything out of my mouth that could potentially jeopardise that. His absence left a hole inside my soul, which I would spend my whole life trying to fill.

My mum's struggles with men led me to try to seek the exact opposite of the dreadful characters I had been surrounded by as a child. I had seen men who were scary, controlling, violent – but thankfully I remained hopeful that there were men out there who could be kind, caring, dependable and hard-working. Much of my mother's life was dominated by men and, although I wanted mine to be different, I would later find that pattern repeating itself. Except, instead, I would seek protective, safe men to shield me from the harshness of the world. (Spoiler: it didn't really work. But we'll get into that later).

*

It wasn't until I was in my twenties that I started having flashbacks of that day on the beach. I was training to be a midwife, working at a hospital to get my clinical hours. There was student housing near the hospital, and my shifts would often end late, so I'd have to walk down a very dark and isolated route in order to get back to my lodgings. I started having panic attacks. I felt almost paralysed sometimes and would stand outside the hospital, not knowing what to do. I would go back into the hospital and beg a security guard to walk me the five minutes it took to get home – but there wasn't always someone available. Sometimes, I ran the whole way home and would reach my little box room, panting, shaking and crying. I didn't know what was wrong with me. My boyfriend at the time was living in another country for work and I would call him in hysterics, as he tried to soothe me through the phone, helpless.

I didn't know what was happening but my body had certainly been triggered. Being alone and vulnerable night after night had reignited the terror I'd felt that day, when my mum had been rendered completely powerless. Slowly but surely, the memories of what had happened when I was four started flooding back. The perfect white sand. The whisper of the waves. The tranquillity broken by the sound of screams.

I became obsessed with piecing together what had happened. I started trying to research rapes in the country and the year it happened. I was angry, and felt a huge sense of injustice that this man had got away with what he'd done. For a moment, I thought I might be able to find him, but this notion quickly evaporated when I realised I had very little information. I also knew I didn't have the emotional stability to delve any deeper. And, anyway, what did I think I was going to do when I found him? Still, I didn't want to bring up my memories with my mum. I didn't want to cause her any further hurt or heartbreak. So I tried my best to bury those memories deep inside my consciousness and get on with my life.

What I didn't realise, at the time, was that I wasn't alone in carrying around this burden of trauma. Most of us have something painful that eats away at us, and rears its head when we least expect it. Often, it can manifest in the way we react to situations. When we struggle to trust. When we're being 'irrational'. When we completely shut down and disconnect from our emotions. According to mental health charity Mind, emotional and psychological trauma can refer to the events that leave marks on us, but it can also refer to how we're affected by our experiences. Everyone processes trauma differently; one person could be deeply traumatised by an event that would pass another by, and vice versa. Trauma is incredibly complicated, which makes it so hard to understand. I know now that I was experiencing something like post-traumatic stress, an affliction I had only ever associated with veterans returning from war. But, actually, it's a common, normal and even adaptive response to experiencing a traumatic event. And for every one in three people who has had a traumatic experience, this can become even more severe and recurrent, which could lead to a PTSD diagnosis.

An experience of sexual assault, like I had, can deeply impact a person's life – and especially how they view sex. But there are numerous other traumatic kinds of events that leave their marks in small (and sometimes big) ways too. Take, for example, walking down the street as a young girl. I remember walking in my school uniform and, from as young as seven or eight, being catcalled and wolf-whistled, approached or intimidated. I felt like a gazelle heading into the wilderness, knowing that a tiger or lion could pounce at any minute. Experiencing this from such a young age instilled a sense of fear in me – I would walk with keys between my knuckles and, when I got older, pretend to be on the phone for the duration of my journey. If I saw a man walking towards me, I'd cross the road, while simultaneously imagining the possibility that I could die right there and then.

I know I'm not alone. These formative experiences are almost rites of passage for women. This all became crystal-clear when a woman named Sarah Everard went missing in London in March 2021, when she was walking home from seeing friends. As we all waited with bated breath to find out what happened to her, there was an outpouring of stories from women online – women whose trauma of walking the streets in fear had been reawakened. A few days later, a serving police officer named Wayne Couzens was arrested on suspicion of murder. It felt like every woman's worst fears had been realised, and we lit candles in her honour.

The fear didn't come from nowhere – according to a recent YouGov poll for UN Women, 7 out of 10 women had experienced some form of sexual harassment in public, half of all women experienced catcalling, and 37% of women had been groped or faced unwelcome touching. I remember a man once following me on my way home from school, and I had to knock on the door of a stranger's house to deter him from continuing. And according to that poll, I'm one of a third of all women who have been physically followed. These incidents might seem small, and you could simply say that those men meant no harm, and they would never *actually* assault a woman. Maybe they aren't all rapists and killers, but it's disgusting that there are so many men out there who clearly get a kick out of seeing women afraid; who enjoy using their power in this way. But, to be honest, I think it's a much bigger, deeper problem: we live in a culture where men are able to get away with predatory behaviour. I truly believe catcalling and street harassment is where it starts, and sexual assault and even murder is where it ends.

But it doesn't just happen on the streets. In fact, it's unthinkably common for women to experience sexual trauma at the hands of men they trust and believe they love. Like my mum, almost 1 in 3 women aged 16–59 will experience domestic abuse in their lifetime (according to a report by End Violence Against Women 2020/21). That's a horrifically high number. And it worsened during the pandemic; according to a BBC report, Refuge recorded an average of 13,162 calls and messages to its National Domestic Abuse helpline every month between April 2020 and February 2021 – up more than 60% on the average number of monthly contacts at the start of 2020.

As a result, Refuge made nearly 4,500 referrals to refuges across the country, enabling women to flee abusive partners (although it's awful to think just how many women weren't able to escape).

It can feel like women are literally unsafe everywhere. On the streets, in their homes, and in public spaces. I doubt I'd be able to find a woman who doesn't have a story to tell. I can remember countless occasions throughout my life when I would be chatted up in a bar or club and felt scared, trying to act friendly and not come across as too aggressive with my 'no' in case he turned nasty. I remember being pulled upstairs, despite my protestations, into the VIP area of a club by a well-known DJ, only to be saved by me vomiting all over his shoes. I remember men telling me to smile and cheer up, as if the only reason my face exists is to make random losers feel comfortable. I have had my bum slapped and faced angry, offensive comments like 'you're ugly anyway' when I told them I wasn't interested. This isn't abnormal. I'm sure most women can't even pinpoint the specific times this has happened to them, because it's just so frequent.

Many women simply roll our eyes over these kinds of occurrences, even though the trauma – built up from dealing with this on such a regular basis – can run deep. I know that, throughout my youth, I always believed that the only kind of 'rape' was non-consensual penetrative sex, and, even then, there were levels of severity. A woman who was dragged into an alleyway was more of a 'victim' than a woman whose boyfriend got on top of her while she was passed out drunk. Most of the time, we were taught that women get themselves into dangerous situations, and they should be held accountable for that.

I think this is probably why I didn't think I deserved any sympathy when I was sexually assaulted in my teens. I had stayed over at a friend's house after a night out. There were a few of us there, and I passed out to sleep on the sofa. At some point during the night, I woke up with my friend's dick in my mouth. And worst of all (in my mind), I didn't stop it or say no. I didn't feel able to. I didn't want to wake the rest of the house up. He had a girlfriend, and I knew her well. I had been drinking and doing drugs that night so I was delirious. Did that actually happen? I couldn't be sure. But over the next few days, the memory came back to me more and more vividly. When I next saw him, I said I had a vague recollection of something happening. He simply smiled, and said that nothing had. Despite occasionally seeing him over the years, it was never mentioned again.

Sadly, this kind of thing is common too. Not only have I heard too many stories to count, but the statistics show this too: in England and Wales, it's estimated that over half a million women are raped or sexually assaulted each year. And, terribly, mixed-race women like myself are the most over-represented group within that. We experience over four times the numbers of rapes than white women, and Black women double that of white women. I'm sure this is no coincidence. If rape and sexual assault is born from deep sexism and misogyny, then committing these acts against Black and mixed-race women stems from racism too. It's a reminder that our bodies, and our sexuality, mean nothing to a lot of men.

Like so many other women, I didn't want to make a fuss, because I convinced myself it really wasn't that bad. It wasn't *rape*. Was it? Plus, I blamed myself for what happened. I was intoxicated at the time. I didn't remember the details – like how it started or how long it lasted. I felt like it was my fault because I didn't object. I felt deeply ashamed of what I believed my role in it had been. This mentality goes some way to explaining why so many women don't report instances of sexual assault – according to the Office of National Statistics, almost a third of women will tell no one. The most common reasons they found were embarrassment (like me) as well as thinking the police wouldn't help, or that they wouldn't be believed. And this is hardly an unfounded worry – you only have to look at the proportion of sexual assault charges that actually lead to justice. According to that report by End Violence Against Women, in 2019/20 reported rapes stood at 55,259, but there were 2,102 prosecutions and only 1,439 convictions. No wonder women don't see the point.

In fact, the process of pressing charges can be hugely traumatic in itself, with women's sexual preferences and sexual history often aired in court as if it is in any way relevant. I've even heard instances of women's knickers being held up in court, as if the underwear someone wears is somehow the root cause of their assault. Then there's the fact that women from low-income or ethnic minority backgrounds are simply not listened to, with the odds in the justice system stacked against them. As much as Sarah Everard's case shook me to the core, I wondered whether it would have received quite as much media attention had it been someone who was mentally ill or addicted to drugs. If she had been a Black woman or from a working-class background. In fact, there was a noticeable lack of coverage for days after the alleged murder of primary school teacher Sabina Nessa in September 2021. I'm pretty sure it had something to do with the fact she wasn't white. That she wasn't the 'perfect' victim.

Our society has a tendency to victim-blame, and I'm tired of it. There are still people who seem to question why a woman was walking alone, why she was drunk, why she was wearing a short skirt – as if men simply 'can't help themselves'. For one, what does this teach men? That they're weak and unable to control their urges? And what does it teach women? That, by making one wrong move, our lives are disposable, and any inflicted trauma is simply what we deserve? I internalised this idea, blaming myself for a man's penis ending up in my mouth. But I didn't consent. I was asleep, for fuck's sake. We attach so much shame around the circumstances of sexual assault, but, in my opinion, what state the woman was in is utterly irrelevant. It doesn't matter if she was pissed out of her mind, if she was naked or worked as a prostitute – if you don't explicitly consent to a sexual act, then it's a crime committed against you. And any sexual act can inflict trauma, so they all deserve to be treated with a similar level of shock and disgust.

The problem is, women's trauma is so common and yet so often downplayed. We question our own minds and morality; we believe that perhaps our memories are playing tricks on us, or that we behaved badly, encouraged them somehow and deserved everything that happened to us. Or, we think what happened to us wasn't really that bad, and we should probably just get over it. Sexual trauma is inflicted upon us, and yet we harbour so much shame around it. It makes us believe we are dirty or wrong. This means it can take even longer for us to process, and it can reappear later in our lives, like when I was triggered by that isolated walk home from the hospital. It can appear in how our minds and bodies respond, deep inside our subconscious.

'Common ways trauma can manifest for people include a myriad of emotional responses,' explained registered clinical psychologist Dr Roberta Babb when I sat down with her. 'These can be experienced as feeling anxious, depressed, ashamed, confused, guilty, angry or even numb. Some people may experience physical reactions such as upset stomachs, headaches, muscle and body aches and disturbed sleep. It may also manifest as flashbacks to, or nightmares about, the traumatic experience. For others, they may avoid people, events, situations or experiences that remind them of the trauma, and become hypervigilant to potential dangers.'

It's interesting to learn that trauma can stay dormant for such a long time, and appear many years later. We might not even connect these symptoms with our experiences, as our bodies can often react in ways we don't consciously understand.

*

It has taken me a long time to process my own traumas from my childhood. I'd be lying if I said it has been an easy journey. Everyone is different, and we all need different things to help ourselves heal. But it *is* important to try to process our traumas, no matter how painful it is to do so.

'Unresolved trauma can affect a person's mental health, sense of self, well-being and relationships,' said Dr Babb. 'It can also impact a person's sense of agency, safety and security. People can also develop maladaptive ways of coping with difficulties and stress, such as addictive or compulsive behaviours, or even self-injurious behaviours.'

Working through trauma will look different for everyone, but Dr Babb notes that the most important thing for everyone to remember is that 'trauma is a subjective experience, and your emotional responses are normal and valid. Any reaction to a traumatic situation is appropriate. Traumatic reactions are a normal response to an abnormal situation, experience or event.'

Now, I can connect better with that little girl on the beach. I understand how scared, confused and sad she was, and I know that she will always be a part of me.

In many ways, I'm still grappling with the impact it's had on my life – and particularly my sexual journey. I grew up wary of men; I understood that they could be violent and cruel. I thought the only way to guarantee my safety and security in life was to make one of the good ones happy. Essentially, men were an omnipresent force within my life – I was afraid of them, but I also wanted to please them. Of course, I don't think this mindset comes just from experiencing trauma – the misogynistic world we live in has meant that thinking this way is a survival tactic for many women. But I do think my early experiences heightened those feelings.

Witnessing sex in its most shocking, brutal form at such a tender age – when my brain was still going through the earliest stages of development – imprinted a damaging idea about what sex means into my innocent mind. That it was a power imbalance. That it was something a man could take from you. That it was something oppressive, and harsh. Our earliest introduction to sex should be joyful, and my childhood robbed that from me.

I grew up with an extremely blurry idea of what consent should be. I thought 'not consenting' meant actively saying no, meant protesting, meant trying to escape and pushing someone away. To be honest, I think this has been the over-arching notion for such a long time, and I know older generations still often view consent in this way. But thankfully it seems that things are changing – there is much more emphasis now on 'enthusiastic consent'; that if someone doesn't emphatically say 'yes', then essentially they are saying 'no'. So if they're completely wasted, that's a big 'no'. And if they're asleep, that's an even bigger 'no'.

A big point, as Dr Babb reminded me, is that consent is dynamic and can change at any time during a situation. 'It involves active communication and an ongoing process of talking and explicitly reviewing decisions made, as well as discussing the boundaries of what each person involved is comfortable and not comfortable with.'

This is something I try to integrate into my sex life now. Conversations with myself and my partner before, during and after sex are a complete non-negotiable for me. I need very clear communication to help me feel safe and wanted, to understand what my partner needs, and to guide them towards what I need and desire. Expressing any fears or worries before you initiate intimacy will help with relaxation, expressing what you want and what they want will enable you to establish whether they are in line with your boundaries. And making sure you communicate exactly what your boundaries are is crucial. If you don't want your hair pulled, say it. If you don't like being touched in a certain place, say that too. And if you know there are some definite no-no's, ensure you say it before you get started.

This might all sound like a buzzkill, to describe everything in such matter-of-fact terms, but I've actually found it can be fucking sexy. Critically consenting as you go along – with comments like: can I do this? Does this feel good? Are you enjoying this? Do you want me to do this more or do you want me to do something else? All of that is a real turn-on. I mean, who doesn't get turned on by knowing that their partner is having the best time? It's a win-win for everyone involved, but weirdly we've collectively decided that communication during sex removes the spontaneity and the fun. I've found the opposite can be true. You can integrate consent beautifully and carefully into every facet of your interaction. It doesn't have to be abrasive or formal. In fact, I think speaking in this way can even deepen intimacy and connection. And it's so much more important to prioritise consent over spontaneity.

It's reassuring that courses on consent are now being offered to men in many schools, universities and workplaces, and in some places, like Oxford University, they're compulsory. After all, the onus shouldn't be on women to say 'no' and refuse; it should be on men to make sure they're not being complete and utter assholes. The suggestion that men are completely unable to read signals and check in with their sexual partners to ensure they're definitely consenting really doesn't give them the credit they deserve. As I've said before – despite my terrible experiences with the men I grew up with, I have always had faith in men-kind. I know they can unlearn the toxic conditioning they've been taught. And I know there are many, many men out there who are good. (Thank fuck – otherwise we'd all be screwed.)

I'm also heartened that our culture is shifting what it considers to be sexual assault. 'Stealthing', which is when a man removes a condom without consent, is now considered a form of rape (and was spotlighted in Michaela Coel's incredible dark comedy, *I May Destroy You*). 'Upskirting', the act of taking pictures underneath women's skirts, was made illegal in 2019, with offenders facing two years of jail-time – thanks to the work of activist Gina Martin, who had this horrible experience at a music festival. Some changes to the justice system are underway – the 'rough sex defence', whereby lawyers could argue a defendant was having rough sex with a victim, therefore making their death an accident, was officially banned in 2021. Considering the BDSM space is founded on the idea of consent, it's atrocious that men have, in the past, been able to use this as a (literal) get-out-of-jail-free card.

While judicial developments are positive, none of this can help with the psychological damage of sexual trauma, which can last a lifetime and ripple through the generations. It was only recently that I decided to speak to my mum about what happened on that beach. For the first time, we started to tackle what happened to both of us in some joint counselling sessions. Despite the pain, it has been healing to recollect what was previously left unspoken.

When my girls are older, I'm hopeful that rates of sexual assault will have drastically declined. We have a lot of work to do in order to get there, and I think we need to hand the baton over to men to make the necessary change happen. Us women have done all we can to speak (scream) about the long-lasting trauma of assault, but there's only so far it will go without an all-over cultural shift. Men need to stand up and make their voices heard. Can we get there? I don't know, but I'm eternally optimistic.

In the meantime, I will continue to try to grow from my own traumas. My experiences have shaped how I viewed my role as a woman, how I viewed men, what I thought I wanted, and what I thought I deserved. I blamed myself for what happened to my mum, and to me, and this unnoticeable shame sank underneath my skin and – I believe – held me back from feeling the full spectrum of sexual pleasure for a very long time. It's unsurprising, really, when my introduction to sex was shrouded in pain. It took many years to unravel the damage that trauma caused. I'm still working on it.

It makes me sad when I think about how many single acts of cruelty have reverberated through generations of women. How the insidious nature of what it means to be a man can ruin so many women's lives. Their joy. Their potential. Sexual trauma is woven into the fabric of woman-hood. It might be invisible, but I know it's there. Which is why I want to talk about my experiences, even when it's scary and my heart feels like it might jump out of my chest. Because I know that by sharing our pain, we can find comfort in other people's stories too.

If this chapter has triggered you, or stirred up emotions of your own traumas – I am so sorry. You shouldn't have had to experience that. It wasn't your fault. And you didn't deserve it. That heavy burden of shame you're carrying? It shouldn't be your load to lift. It doesn't belong to you. Please know that you are whole, not broken. You are capable and deserving of happiness, and you are not dirty or sullied. You are as bright and beautiful as the day you were born and those scars that you carry around only make your soul more incredible, more interesting and more human. Most of all, I am with you. We all are.

What I've learned about trauma and healing:

- Not talking about your trauma doesn't make it go away. Find someone who makes you feel safe, and talk to them. It doesn't have to be a therapist, just a trusted friend or relative who will listen and not judge. But be careful not to offload on someone without their expressed permission, and warn them if the topics could be triggering.

- If you are in a financial position to do so, I'd really recommend seeking therapy. It's the best way to unpack your traumas and learn how to move through them in a

safe way. For more information about how to find a
therapist, visit nhs.uk, or mind.org.uk.

- There are some great books you can read to inspire
  healing. I recommend *How to Do the Work* by Dr Nicole
  LePera and *A Radical Awakening* by Dr Shefali Tsabary.

- As much as trauma can make you turn inward, and feel so
  alone, there are so many people out there who have
  experienced something similar and understand exactly
  how you're feeling. It might seem scary, but talking about
  my experiences openly on social media has helped me to
  find like-minded people who understand what I've been
  through. It really helps.

2

Virginity

The first time I became aware of my sexual power, I was around 11 years old. I was in the supermarket with my mum, dressed in leggings and a crocheted knit-top; the kind where you could see through the holes if you looked very closely. There was a middle-aged man in the shop with his wife and children, who kept looking over, and I could've sworn he was following me around. I remember thinking, 'wow, he's obsessed with me.' It felt strangely exciting and intriguing. Looking back now, I realise it was pretty fucked up that this much older man was clearly very interested in an obviously much younger girl. But I learned an important lesson that day: that enticing and influencing men held a special kind of power.

Our society, it seems to me, is obsessed with young girls' transition into womanhood. We have this idea that girls are innocent and angelic, but as soon as they start to develop breasts and curves, they become temptresses. Subconsciously, I know I absorbed this idea. As I started my period and began to grow, teachers told me to unroll my school skirt to make it longer, so as not to distract the boys in my class. I knew that if I wore a low-cut top or wore shorts in the street, I would receive unwanted attention from men. Before I knew what sex actually was, I understood the politics of it. With my new 'womanly' body came great responsibility. The onus was on me, as a girl, to be careful about how I presented myself, and not to give myself away too easily. My childhood had taught me that men were something to be feared, but I also learned – from that day in the supermarket, and many times afterwards – that they could be used and influenced.

There was something about that power dynamic that fizzed with excitement and possibility. Whatever sex entailed, I knew it was the ultimate sign of womanhood and maturity, but also that it was forbidden and dirty; one wrong move, and you could be forever sullied. It was like a mythical creature; I was fascinated by it, but scared by it, but also really fucking fascinated by it. I think it's natural, especially when you're young, to gravitate towards that kind of piping-hot mythology. So I rolled my skirt up as soon as my teachers were looking the other way, applied lipstick (complete with dark liner around the edge of my lips, which was all the rage), and found that the reactions of boys, and men, could be intoxicating.

I started my sexual journey at a young age. Of course, I didn't think I was young at the time: as children often do, I believed I was independent and grown-up beyond my years. I had my first kiss that same summer, before starting secondary school. With a group of friends at my local swimming pool, we played a version of spin the bottle where we took turns to snog under the water. I probably kissed five boys that day, and although the sensation was muffled by the taste of chlorine, it was electrifying. None of the adults could see what we were doing underwater, and it felt risky and fun (especially when I got to kiss one of the 'hot' boys with cool, floppy hair, who everyone fancied – you know the kind).

Shortly after, in year 7, I had my first one-on-one encounter with a boy – let's call him Luke. My friends whispered in lessons that he fancied me, and it felt like my greatest accomplishment. To be chosen, wanted, by a *boy*? I'd made it. I'm not sure whether I liked him, or if I was drunk on the idea that he liked me, but we stole fevered glances across the playground and passed notes in Maths. Eventually, we made out in an alleyway on our way home from school. I don't even think his hands touched me but he shoved his tongue inside my mouth, making a swirling motion that mimicked a washing machine. It was gross. In my favourite movies, like *Pretty Woman* and *Flashdance*, kissing seemed romantic. It was the precursor to 'doing it', the first sign of mature connection. By contrast, this kiss felt sloppy and awkward. I wonder whether he was actually enjoying it himself; he was probably just as clueless as I was. Either way, I think we were both under the illusion that this dynamic – boys being active, girls being passive – was what sexual contact was all about.

It didn't help that this idea was perpetuated in the curriculum. Sex education in my school was pretty standard for the early nineties – it was sparse, infrequent, but when it did happen, it focused on how babies are made and little else. There was nothing in the syllabus about feelings or pleasure, at least not for girls. 'Sex', in these lessons, was defined solely as heterosexual, penetrative: man and woman, penis inside vagina. I think multiple generations have had this same experience: we were taught that the purpose was to get pregnant, and that required a man to orgasm, which seemed to be the only thing that mattered. I'm sure masturbation was mentioned, but only in the context of, 'boys need to do this, they can't help themselves'. I genuinely believed that self-pleasure was reserved only for my male peers. Did we even learn what a clitoris was, let alone that orgasms existed for women? I don't think that was ever on the agenda.

In one lesson, we were encouraged to anonymously submit questions to our teacher. Although our classes presented sex as biological and matter-of-fact, this kind of secrecy made clear that sex was taboo and shameful. As my teacher went through the questions – like whether you can get pregnant from a blow job – there was a lot of sniggering. It was so uncomfortable. In some lessons, boys and girls were divided into separate groups. Our teachers said it was so we could feel more comfortable, but I always wondered what the boys were being told that we weren't. It seemed like we both had separate responsibilities and goals when it came to sex – that we were on two different teams. For boys: make sure you enjoy yourself enough to ejaculate. For girls: your only purpose is to get pregnant, but also try not to get pregnant. The idea that sex should be a collaboration, where both parties thought about enjoyment and protection, seemed an alien concept.

Virginity

We were taught about safe sex – we all tried putting condoms on cucumbers – but the overarching message at my Catholic school was that abstaining from sex was ultimately the best way to protect ourselves from the myriad dangers it presented. I was coming of age at the height of the AIDs crisis, and I distinctly remember the advertising campaign featuring a tombstone that read in bold letters: 'don't die of ignorance'. It was the scariest shit I had ever seen. Our lessons taught us that STDs were enemy number two. Enemy number one, though, was undoubtedly teenage pregnancy. The *Mean Girls* quote, 'don't have sex, because you will get pregnant . . . and die!' pretty much sums up the messaging we received. I believed that getting 'knocked up' while I was still in school uniform was the worst possible thing I could do. No one wanted to be that girl with the bump underneath her polo shirt. The messaging was always targeted towards us girls; we were warned not to 'fall' pregnant, as if it was a punishment we could bring upon ourselves by not behaving morally. Where did the sperm come from? Well, that was irrelevant. Women carry the babies, therefore it became our responsibility to prevent it happening.

When I was in year 9, one of my friends confided in me during a breaktime at school, in panicked whispers, that she might be pregnant. I convinced her to get a pregnancy test on our way home, and she came to my house so we could do it together. We stood huddled in the bathroom, discussing what she might do if the result came back positive, and when the two little lines appeared, showing she was pregnant, we were stunned into silence. I remember thinking it was the most dramatic thing to ever happen. Being part of it was weirdly exciting, and I was really fucking glad it wasn't me. Although I felt so sorry for her, safe sex had been drilled into us; we knew how important it was to use protection so I berated her for being so stupid. She ended up having a secret abortion. Looking back, I regret reacting the way I did. I had internalised the misogynistic idea that the blame was all hers. I didn't consider the fact she was dating an older man, who had convinced her not to use condoms because he preferred having sex without. She was vulnerable and susceptible, yet I had decided it was all her fault. Although I did support her and stand by her, I could have been a better friend to her.

Blaming and shaming girls, though, was the norm. This was especially true for girls who we decided were 'too' sexual. Initially, the first girls who'd had sex in our year group were idolised. We viewed them as mature and sophisticated; they had seen something of the adult world that the rest of us hadn't. But, if they continued to explore their sexual selves, if they started having sex with too many different people, they were knocked off their pedestals with a thump. Perceived as dirty and disgusting, they were labelled 'slags', which was one of the worst insults you could receive. That, and 'bucket crotch', a horrible term to suggest that a woman's vagina would be too big and baggy if she had too much sex, rendering her useless in pleasuring any men in future. The whole idea was absurd; if a girl had sex every day with the same partner in a long-term relationship, would that not also make her a 'bucket crotch'? Apparently not. It was ridiculous, but I was afraid of it, so I believed it. I didn't want to end up like those girls. No one did. The boys in our school would name and shame them, shouting in lessons that so-and-so got fingered, and so-and-so shagged two boys in one night. Again, the boys' roles in these sexual experiences were afterthoughts. While girls could be ruined for having too much sex, boys were, at worst, let off the hook ('that's just what they do,' people would say) or, at best, held up as legends. Now, I see this slut-shaming double standard for what it is: deeply ingrained sexism and misogyny. At the time, I thought it was just the way things were.

And, yet, alongside the potential for ruined reputations, teen motherhood and even death, I was entranced by the idea of sex. As the curriculum only scratched the surface, and without the ease of the internet to lean on, I was forced to collect scraps of information about sex from wherever I could find them. I remember overhearing my mum's friend talking about a man licking every inch of her body. I was fascinated by it; the idea that a woman's body could be something delicious for a man, like an ice cream. From hushed conversations with friends, I learned about the gradient of sexual experiences. There was a lot of talk about bases. Does anyone actually know which base means what? I still don't, but I know they involved snogging, groping, fingering, wanking off, blow jobs, and licking out; a series of boxes to tick before progressing to the real thing. With each of these, it was very important to master them; to perfect the ideal hand motion or tongue movements. For this, I turned to magazines (I was especially intrigued by *More!* magazine's Position of the Fortnight; the positions all looked virtually impossible but I was desperate to try them) and porn (but more on that later).

Unsurprisingly, all these formative lessons created a confusing and conflicting picture of sex, and my role in it. I knew I was supposed to be pure but sexy, knowledgeable but innocent. Pleasuring boys was a priority, but so was protecting my reputation – and doing both at the same time seemed like a tricky balancing act. But one thing I was certain of was that my first experience of sex was important.

I had internalised the idea that my virginity was something sacred, like a precious fruit that could be given to a man as a gift. This idea is a tale as old as time. In many cultures and religions around the world, female virginity is glorified and fetishised. I'm not quite sure why everyone is so fixated on it, but in feminist writer Jessica Valenti's book, *The Purity Myth*, she cites the theory of historian (and author of *Virgin: The Untouched History*), Hanne Blank. 'Blank posits that a long-standing historical interest in virginity is about establishing paternity (if a man marries a virgin, he can be reasonably sure the child she bears is his) and about using women's sexuality as a commodity,' she writes. 'Either way, the notion has always been deeply entrenched in patriarchy and male ownership.' Throughout history, it has been used against women – pre-marital sex (even if non-consensual) could lead to a woman's 'ruin'; her essential feminine innocence forever destroyed. By contrast, male virginity doesn't hold the same currency. You only have to read a Shakespeare play, watch *Bridgerton* or read any history book to know that unmarried men would regularly attend brothels and explore sex before settling down. And that idea has continued even now – virginity for men is pretty irrelevant, except perhaps, to laugh at them if they still possess it (like in *American Pie* and *The 40-Year-Old Virgin*). Women are pressured to keep it, and men are pressured to lose it.

The whole concept of female virginity is entangled with ideas of purity, which I find so problematic. Just look at the language we use when talking about it: we say we 'lose' virginity, as if we're discarding something treasured. We talk about 'deflowering', as if women's vaginas are like precious flowers that have been crushed. It's weird! In *The Purity Myth*, Jessica Valenti wrote: 'Women are led to believe that our moral compass lies somewhere between our legs.' I nodded in furious recognition when I read this, because that's exactly how I thought about it when I was in school; that how I behaved with my body would either make me 'good' or 'bad'. It turns out that this notion was first identified by the esteemed founder of psychoanalysis Sigmund Freud, and is known as the 'Madonna–Whore Dichotomy'; it's the idea that men believe women can only be 'good' pure madonnas, or 'bad' promiscuous whores. I definitely grew up believing that there was no place in-between.

And I was preoccupied with being good; I'd built my whole identity around it. Although I was friends with the popular group at school who were loud and confident, I was quieter; I kept my head down and tried not to cause any trouble. Since my home life could be volatile, I didn't want to do anything to add to the load. Enacting my role as a 'good girl' was very important to me. But of course, this was the 1990s, so I knew that waiting for marriage to lose my virginity (the ultimate 'good girl' act) was unrealistic. But having sex within a long-term, committed relationship felt like the next best thing.

I met my first boyfriend when I was just 13 years old. Let's call him Jack. He was seven years older than me and worked in a local shop. He had brown skin, jet black hair, and – crucially – he chain-smoked and drove his own car. I thought he was the definition of cool. We met in my local park and, at first, I lied about my age, telling him I was 16. When I revealed the truth just a couple of weeks later, he didn't seem to care in the slightest, and we continued seeing each other. When I look back on that relationship now, I realise just how vulnerable I was, and that I wasn't being protected. My mum expressed reservations at first but was preoccupied with a new relationship closely followed by newborn twins, and her boyfriend at the time seemed to think that being with an older man was good for me. According to my mum, he actually approved of my relationship because he thought older men were 'less horny' than teenagers. No one seemed to bat an eyelid at our age difference.

It seems outrageous to look back on now, but it's unsurprising. At the time, society didn't really seem to object to the idea of younger girls dating older men. Although the age of consent was 16, it wasn't until the Sexual Offences Act of 2003 that statutory rape – which stipulates that sex with anyone under the age of 16 does not count as consensual – was defined as 'sexual activity with a child' versus 'unlawful sexual intercourse', meaning heftier penalties for those found guilty. When I was coming of age, ideas about 'grooming' young, vulnerable girls weren't really discussed. There was a prevailing view in society that young girls could and did have full control over their sexual power. This way of thinking is probably why it took so long for the sexual abuse allegations to be uncovered in the famous case of the Rochdale paedophile ring – because it was believed that the girls (as young as 13 years old) were consenting to prostitution. It's pretty fucked up.

Clearly, despite being written in 1955, the ideas and eroticism from Vladimir Nabokov's cult novel *Lolita* – about a man who is obsessed with a 12-year-old girl – seemed to live on, and these kinds of relationships were glamorised and fetishised in popular culture. Even my beloved *Pretty Woman* portrayed an 18-year age gap (Julia Roberts was 22 when the movie was filmed, compared to Richard Gere's 41). Although it's not the same as sexualising a child, I still thought these kinds of age differences were impossibly romantic. I didn't think they represented an imbalance of power, and an element of exploitation. It all goes back to that idea of girls becoming sexual fodder as soon as they pass puberty, making big-age-gap relationships – with older men and younger girls – seem socially acceptable.

And so, my friends and I were obsessed with the idea of dating older men. We believed we were far too mature to date boys our own age. After all, we had breasts and curves before some of the boys' voices had broken. We looked down on them and their boyish habits; we thought we were way cooler and far more worldly. When Jack would wait for me outside the school gates in his red Honda Civic,

I felt like I had accomplished something greater than everyone else. At that age, I loved feeling like a fully-grown adult, smoking cigarettes out of his car window and nodding along when he moaned about his boss, and I moaned about having detention. The boys in my class were idiots, I thought: they could play their Game Boys while I got to kiss someone who could grow a beard. Now, I envy those boys. They got to be the age they were, while I was thrust into the adult world before I needed to. Let's face it: before I was ready.

Dating an older man appealed to me even more because it provided an illusion of safety and security that I desperately craved. My only goal in life was to get married, have children and buy a house. Having been raised by a single mother in an unstable household, I yearned for a future that epitomised everything I didn't have: family-oriented; homely; with four kids; a man who adored me and who would provide for his children. I felt sick with jealousy seeing my friends' dads pick them up from parties, or help them with their homework. I was needy for the adoration, love and acceptance I never felt I received from my own dad, who was busy with his other family. I projected that onto my love life; I wanted to find someone who would look after me and protect me.

I thought that would be Jack. Despite his age, he knew that I wanted to hold onto my virginity for as long as possible. He was aware that I'd never had sex before and, although he never directly insinuated that the idea of this excited him, it definitely felt like an extra presence in our relationship. Just like that feeling I had in the supermarket,

Virginity

I imagined that I was clutching onto a magical power and that, once I gave it away, my superpowers would be gone. Instead, we did other 'stuff' – progressing through that gradient of sexual experiences I'd been taught to view as test runs; practice for the main event. Although Jack had more experience than me, he clearly didn't know what he was doing either. Blow jobs were pretty unpleasant (but necessary, I had learned from magazines, to keep him interested) and fingering often felt rough and sore. He liked licking me out but I just didn't get it. Thrusting his tongue inside my vagina did nothing for me, but I lay there staring at the ceiling, and lied when he asked me if I enjoyed it.

Though, there was one occasion – yes, just one – that felt really good. Jack must have been fingering me at an angle that was stimulating my clitoris, because I felt tiny sparks of electricity flowing through my body. For the first time, I felt like I could get truly excited about the idea of sex; I thought, 'if this is how it feels, then no wonder people want to do it all the time'. Just as I was relaxing into it, we heard my mum's footsteps on the landing, so Jack pulled his hand away. I couldn't wait to start again later that night, but no matter how hard we tried, the sparks were gone. I didn't know how to get them back, because I had no idea how or why it felt so good. I didn't even know what my clitoris was, and I'm pretty sure Jack was none the wiser either. I wish I had known what was happening in my body, and had the language to ask for more of it. Instead, I chased that feeling every time he came near my vulva, and I never felt that way again for the whole time we were together.

Feeling Myself

In the end, we waited six months before we had penetrative sex. I knew he was keen for it to happen, but he didn't constantly pester me for it. Though, he carried around condoms in his wallet, just in case. I thought I was a textbook 'good girl' for waiting that long. Six months feels like a lifetime when you're 13. I saved the special occasion for Valentine's Day – my virginity was almost like a gift; a symbol to show how much I loved him. And I really did believe I loved him. This, I felt, was important to ensure my first time wasn't marred by immorality. If it was true love, how could I be branded a slag? To mitigate all the other risks, I secretly went on the pill. I turned the occasion over in my mind almost constantly for the week before: what if he doesn't like it? What if he doesn't want me any more? What if it hurts, and I bleed all over my bed, and my mum finds my stained sheets and knows what I've done? But what if it really is as good as I'd always imagined, and we become more in love than ever before? Whatever way I looked at it, my first time having sex was a big deal; an event that would change my life forever.

When it finally happened, losing my virginity was an anti-climax (quite literally). It was typical, really: Jack fumbled with my bra clasp, accidentally put the condom on the wrong way around and had to replace it with another one (and *he* was supposed to be the experienced one), the first few thrusts were sore, and once I'd stopped wincing from the pain, it was all over. Jack collapsed on top of me and I had the sinking realisation that I had officially 'lost' my virginity. My innocence was gone, and I'd never get it back.

I thought I'd feel transformed, but instead, I thought: 'what the fuck was all the hype about?' Despite the joy and excitement in my imagination, it was dull, not particularly enjoyable or comfortable, and I felt distinctly under-whelmed. Now, of course, I realise this is a very common experience, but at the time, I wondered what was wrong with me. How come everyone else got to have such an amazing experience? Now, I realise, most of the people who said their first time was magical, mind-blowing or life-changing were lying – because they were just as ashamed as I was.

To make matters worse, once I'd done it, I didn't feel I was in a position to say 'no' to Jack, who I stayed with for two more years. Sex felt like a routine, a chore; something I had to get through in order to keep him. How else could I keep hold of the security and stability he offered my life? He supported me when my parents weren't around, and helped me look after my baby sisters. I felt wanted and safe in his arms. Sex, I felt, was simply how I fulfilled my end of the bargain. I didn't think it mattered whether I wanted to do it or not; it was just something that had to be done, like washing the dishes. The idea that I could possibly want more seemed so shameful, so much like the antithesis of the 'good girl' I was trying to be, that I squashed it down altogether. It was almost as if, once I had given away my most prized possession, there was nothing valuable left to hold onto.

I've only recently begun to unpack just how damaging these notions actually are. For one, so many of our prevail-ing ideas about female virginity are outdated and false. I remember being terrified of bleeding, because I had been led to believe that 'popping my cherry' (breaking my hymen) would be like fracturing a part of my identity I'd never get back. I know in some cultures, a torn hymen is used as evidence for a woman's impurity, and in some places, doctors check a woman's hymen is intact before she's allowed to get married. It might not be as extreme as that in the UK, but I certainly believed that my hymen was the physical symbol of my virginity, and therefore my innocence (or lack thereof). But according to Dr Karen Gurney, clinical psychologist, psychosexologist and author of *Mind The Gap*, determining virginity is a myth.

'The hymen, being the thin membrane of skin surrounding the vaginal opening, is something that wears away in its own time,' she told me. 'There is no way to scientifically tell if a woman has had penetrative vaginal sex.'

Plus, the concept of virginity is woefully exclusive and heteronormative. If oral sex and masturbating each other are only reserved as 'foreplay', and the loss of virginity is directly associated with a penis inside a vagina, what does that mean for LGBTQ+ people, who may have never had sexual contact with the opposite sex? Are they all virgins? Plus, I know some men who pinpoint the loss of their virginity to the first time they had an orgasm with a woman. It's hardly surprising, as men are taught in schools to measure their ejaculation as the sign that sex has completed. So if we smashed through the double standard and defined it like that for women – that it only counts if you come – how many women would have lost their virginities the first time they had sex? My guess is, not very many at all.

Virginity

When you look at it like this, you realise virginity is just a social construct. I like to think we've modernised when it comes to sexual freedom, but the prevailing importance placed on virginity, socially, shows we have a long way to go. We think it'll be a moment of cataclysmic change; that we will emerge from it completely transformed. We also believe the way we lose it, and who we lose it to, will have a direct impact on that change. Will you enter into adulthood as a 'good girl' who did everything right? Or a 'bad girl', with twisted morals and a dirty vagina?

The problem is, I spent so much of my energy worrying about how I looked to other people. I wanted my friends to think I was mature and cool. Unlike the conversations I have with my friends now – where we're open about sex toys, orgasms and dissatisfaction – whenever I spoke to my closest friends about sex then, it was always slightly boastful. We'd confide in each other about our latest sexual escapades, not with any sense of vulnerability, but to say 'look how fucking mature I am'. I don't think we were ever emotionally in touch with ourselves enough to even think about, or ask, whether we were enjoying it or not. It was never about that. My teenage years were never about me; what my wants and needs were. Having wants and needs, in itself, was too shameful to admit. The main question that dominated my mind was: 'how am I coming across to other people?' I do believe this is an affliction that girls, in particular, tend to suffer. I have a theory that boys grow up seeing themselves as they are, while girls grow up seeing themselves predominantly through the lens of how others view them.

Feeling Myself

I wanted Jack to think I was sexy and worldly (but also innocent and pure). I wanted to be a 'good girl' for my mum and my teachers, and a legend among my friends. Gripping onto all these conflicting mirror images of myself was hard, and it weighed me down. Most of all, I wanted everyone to see me as a grown-up, not a child. Now I realise just how redundant that effort was. Having sex doesn't equate to growing up. I still had plenty of growing up to do.

For many years, I regretted how my first time happened, because I had placed far too much emphasis on it as a life-changing moment. There were no fireworks; no magical connection. I didn't even know my way around my own body, and I certainly didn't have the language to ask for what I wanted, so it's hardly surprising that I was dissatisfied. The mythology surrounding losing my virginity in the 'right' way created so much unnecessary pressure – it was destined to be disappointing.

But I also know now that I shouldn't have even been in that scenario in the first place. I was far too young to consent to sex, especially with an older man. Jack and I had a long and (I believed) loving relationship, so it feels very messy and strange to admit that. I had been enthusiastic about having sex, and I believed I was ready. Sex should never be frowned upon if it's between two consenting adults. The problem is, I wasn't a consenting adult. I was more vulnerable than I realised, confused by all the conflicting expectations placed on me, and still very much a child. Should I have been better protected? If one of my daughters ever came home at the age I was then, with a man 7.5 years older than her, I know I would hit the roof. I'd call the police, and do whatever I could to make her realise it's not okay. But things were different back then. I don't think anyone knew any better.

*

If we want to change things, so that our kids don't grow up with the same damaging ideals about virginity and sex, I strongly believe that we should start having conversations with children about sex as young as possible. Before they catch an old man staring at them in the supermarket. Before they feel twinges of desire. Before a kid rams a tongue down their throat. And definitely before they watch porn. The more children know about sex, the more equipped they will be to make informed choices – and the safer they will be.

Today's world feels like even more of a minefield for kids to learn about sex. If I was able to easily collect unhelpful information about sex in the 1990s, then today's kids will be bombarded with it. Over a third of children aged 8–11 have their own smartphone, and 21% are already on social media by this age. And with image-sharing apps like Instagram, Snapchat and TikTok popular among youngsters, damaging messages about sex can be spread alarmingly easily. In fact, in 2021, there were reports about a sickening trend on TikTok encouraging viewers to attack women on 24 April for 'National Rape Day'. It got so much traction that I received a letter about this from my daughters' school warning parents. It's utterly disgusting, and it really makes me worry about how quickly misogynistic and sexually abusive content can spread.

The rise of smartphones has also led to a new phenomenon of revenge porn. At school, if I were to take a naked picture of myself, I'd have to borrow my mum's clunky camera and then get it developed. There was no way I'd let those images be processed and seen by random strangers in the photo shop. But today, all it takes is a quick click for explicit images to be taken, with the belief that they will stay private, before being spread around schools at an alarming rate, resulting in bullying and trauma. It was reported by the *Guardian* that, in 2019, 541 children were victims of revenge porn – some as young as 10 years old. It's shocking and deeply worrying.

That said, though, I'm hopeful that today's teenagers will be growing up with more well-rounded knowledge about sex than I did. In 2017, the government announced that sex education would be compulsory in all schools in England (previously, it was only compulsory in council-run schools, meaning some schools could swerve teaching it altogether). A new curriculum launched in 2020, which incorporates diverse family structures – including LGBTQ+ families. Sadly, but perhaps unsurprisingly, integrating homosexuality in the curriculum caused a lot of controversy. But I think it's brilliant that children will be growing up with a greater understanding of relationships, which extends beyond simply men and women making babies.

However, there's still an ongoing campaign to get female pleasure onto the curriculum, and the lessons our kids learn about sex still bob along at the surface. If we want our kids to grow up with less shame than we did about natural, human desire, we need to teach it on the curriculum. Personally, I'd like to see our sex education curriculum mimic that of the Netherlands, which is one of the world's most gender-equal countries. According to an article in *The Atlantic* titled 'How The Dutch Do Sex Ed', the Dutch start compulsory sex education from an even younger age than we do in the UK – from around four – where they learn about reproduction, discovering their own sexual likes and dislikes, and boundaries. Some people might argue that this destroys children's innocence before their time, but I think that instilling an understanding of how natural and important sex is from a young age will reduce shame later down the line. There's also no evidence that Dutch kids end up being sexualised any earlier; they have sex for the first time at roughly the same age as in the UK (the average for both is between 16 and 18), and they have fewer teen pregnancies.

Normalising sex, I think, is fundamental to ensuring kids don't enter into their sexual lives feeling ashamed of their own bodies, and confused by the expectations placed on them. Yes, lots of that would come from improving sex education in schools, but the way we talk about these issues in popular culture makes a massive difference too. I'm grateful that there are more depictions of healthy teen sex on TV and in movies nowadays. I wish I could've watched *Sex Education* on Netflix when I was young; the brilliant comedy drama series covers topics like abortion, vaginismus and peer pressure. There are so many more resources out there if we want to take advantage of them – Brook is an excellent organisation, which provides no-nonsense, honest sex and well-being advice to young people. Their website is full of information that, had I had access to this when I was young, would've made me feel far less alone.

And of course, us parents and guardians do have to take responsibility for how our kids learn about sex – no matter how awkward it can feel sometimes. I'm making a conscious effort to talk about sex with my girls (who are aged 9 and 12 as I write this) as frequently, as honestly, as possible. This sometimes makes me (and them) feel uncomfortable – but I'm trying to push through those icky feelings. This discomfort is ingrained in us, as it was often passed down from our own parents, so we need to get comfortable with this if we want to break the cycle.

When one of my daughters was six, she asked how babies were made for the first time. I would never have considered telling her some kind of fairy tale involving magical storks and mysterious baskets appearing on doorsteps, because I knew that wasn't going to help her in the long run. I've always believed if they are old enough to ask, they are old enough to get the real answers without bullshit stories. That didn't make me any less nervous to tell her the truth though – I really had to swallow my discomfort.

'It happens when a man puts his penis inside a woman's vagina,' I told her. I decided to use the proper terms, too – not infantilising language like 'willy' or 'front-bottom'. If we want to teach our children not to be squeamish or ashamed about body parts, we need to name them just as we would an arm or a leg.

I hoped that might be enough to satisfy her curiosity for now, but she responded with a very insightful question:

'But how does it get in there?' she asked. 'Wouldn't it be squishy?'

'Yes,' I replied, 'he has to let his penis go hard first.'

'How does that happen?' she snapped back.

'Once he gets excited,' I said, 'from having kisses and cuddles.'

'But doesn't it hurt?' she responded. I squirmed slightly, and replied: 'Well, it does sometimes, at first. But a woman releases some vaginal fluid when she gets excited, which helps the penis go in.'

'But doesn't that make a mess?' she responded.

'Yes, yes it bloody does!' I laughed. I was proud of how pragmatic and forthcoming she was in her questions. The thing is, kids are much smarter than we give them credit for. They know if we're trying to hide something, and this can lead to distrust. I want my kids to trust me wholeheartedly, as I never want them to keep secrets when they get older. If my daughters had a sexual experience that made them feel unsafe, I would want them to tell me. Many people think that the best way to keep our kids safe when it comes to sex is to simply tell them not to do it. I understand that response – it can feel easier to bury your head in the sand and pretend something isn't happening. But I couldn't disagree more. Sex is human nature; when we go through puberty, our bodies are gearing up to embrace our sexuality. To deny that, to suggest that children can be shielded from the reality of sex, is so unrealistic.

When I talk about sex with my children, I try hard not to impose my biases and assumptions on them. I don't assume they will only be interested in a certain gender, and I want them to explore that the conventional course of getting married and having kids isn't the only way to be. I want them to know that I'm still learning too. In fact, when I think back to that conversation I had with my daughter, I wish I'd told her about IVF and surrogacy as an alternative way babies are made. It's hard to cover everything in one discussion though, so I try to keep the conversation going. I ask open questions like: How do you feel about sex? What would you like to know? When do you think you'll be ready to have sex? Often, I'm met with eye-rolls and 'Mum, can you stop talking about sex please? You're so embarrassing'. But I'd rather be embarrassing than silent.

I also think it's vital to talk about emotions and feelings. Any discussion of feelings was completely absent from my sex education at school, and from my home life. Everything was always about how I appeared to other people; being mature or worldly or good. I don't think anyone ever asked me: how does that feel for you? Are you enjoying yourself? Is it making you happy? This is a huge part of how I interact with my kids anyway, but when they start exploring their sexual selves, I plan to prioritise these kinds of conversations even more. I know from experience that, often, you don't even know how you feel until you're asked. So keep asking.

When my daughters start having sex – of any kind – for the first time, I will *not* be describing it as 'losing' their virginity. I know I don't have much control over when it happens, or who with – although you can be damn sure I will try to protect them as much as I can from lurking older men. Before it happens, I want to make sure they know that feelings are the most important part of the equation. My girls know (because I won't stop banging on about it) that their virginity is not a physical thing; a piece of treasure to be given away to another person. It's as much for them to enjoy as it is for their partner. They are not commodities, existing purely for the pleasure of other people. Their sense of morality has absolutely nothing to do with who, where, and when they have sex. Their purity and innocence comes from their kindness and empathy, and that will exist long after they have their first sexual partners.

I wish I'd had this kind of messaging when I was young. When I look back on my early sexual experiences, I realise that they shaped my understanding of who I am, what I'm worth, and what sex should be. And the sad part is: I know I'm in the majority here. If you didn't absorb sexist, shame-inducing ideas about sex from your early sexual experiences and formal education, you're very lucky. I'm only just beginning to abandon all those negative messages. It has taken me this long to realise that sex should never feel like an exchange of power, offered from one person to another. Impressing a male partner shouldn't be the central focus. It should always be an equal transaction; a collaboration and partnership. It should never feel like something that is done to you – only *with* you. And most importantly, sex doesn't exist to determine who you are: good, bad, slag, frigid, mature, innocent, madonna, whore. It's there to be enjoyed.

What I've learned about virginity and sex education:

- The whole idea of virginity is bullshit, and we need to get the message out there. Try adjusting your language – you could say that someone 'had their first sexual experience', or had their 'sexual debut'. Changing the language we use can encourage a culture shift.

- As adults, there are gaping holes in our knowledge and we still have so much to learn about sex. I recommend books like *Come as You Are* by Emily Nagoski and *Mind The Gap* by Dr Karen Gurney. We are all on constant learning journeys, and we should never stop our own sexual education.

- It's not solely a school's responsibility to educate our children about sex. We have to fill in the gaps, for example, talking to them about feelings and pleasure.

- It might feel incredibly awkward to talk about sex with your kids, but push past that awkwardness! I recommend talking to them in a neutral and relaxed setting, perhaps using a movie or TV show storyline, or something in the news, as a starting point. I like to initiate difficult conversations in the car; there's no direct eye contact so it doesn't feel so intense. Conversations about sex should be light and relaxed, otherwise it could scare them away.

Virginity

- Exploring your sexuality safely and consensually is not a bad thing – I wish I knew how to do that when I was younger. I think an open and honest dialogue with people I trust would have facilitated this.

- It's never too early to talk to kids about sex – if they're old enough to ask, they're old enough to hear an honest, clear answer. Avoid using silly names for our body parts – they're nothing to be ashamed of, so we can use the correct language.

- Reading books that are inclusive and representative is important for children. I try to ensure that my children have a well-rounded knowledge of all different types of families, sexualities, genders.

3

Porn

Do you remember the first time you saw pornography? I do. I was seven or eight years old, standing in my living room, wearing a thin synthetic My Little Pony nightdress. On the TV, I watched a woman (who I now realise was a stripper) flinging her long blonde hair around and around, as she moved her body in a wave-like motion around a silver pole. I was transfixed; wide-eyed and curious. A local older boy was babysitting me, and he'd invited another boy from our street over. Somehow, they'd found the VHS tapes on my mum's shelves that she'd (clearly unsuccessfully) tried to hide, by labelling them with innocuous film titles. The boys laughed hysterically while the stripper seduced an older man, and proceeded to bounce up and down on his lap, making noises that appeared animal-like to my young ears. I had no idea what was going on but I was intrigued, and from the boys' reaction, I knew there was something thrilling about it. My whole body prickled; I didn't know how or why but there was this really strange feeling that emanated from my stomach. I couldn't work out whether it was a deeply uncomfortable feeling, or whether I liked it.

But I also knew that it was something that was meant to be kept a secret. Once the video was over, I watched the boys as they carefully rewound the VHS to exactly the right location where it had previously ended, placing it back on the shelf in exactly the right spot. I will never know why they decided to play the porn while I was in the room. They were teenagers and I guess they thought it was funny, and wanted to see my reaction. I laughed along with them, to show I was mature and in on the joke. But that evening left a mark on me, piquing my curiosity. I knew that something naughty was hiding in our living room bookcase. I wondered: what was so appealing about it? And why did it need to be concealed?

Over the years that followed, I'd see more of these kinds of images – both accidentally and intentionally – and I gradually understood what they were, and why they seemed so forbidden. I'd find copies of my mum's boyfriends' magazines lying around, which were filled with images of naked women, and people having sex. Sometimes, when my mum was out, I'd take down one of her badly hidden VHS tapes and put it on. Her porn collection was straight out of the 1970s; the men sported mullets and the women had big, bushy pubic hair. The movies usually had some kind of storyline – I recall an orgy made up of ancient Romans, dressed in togas. But the plots always involved some kind of power dynamic – normally a strong, handsome man, and a weak, beautiful damsel in distress. The woman always seemed to be angelic and innocent, but as soon as she started having sex, she transformed into a kind of wild animal. As a young girl set on being 'good', this was fascinating to me. 'So I'm supposed to be good all the time, except when I'm having sex?' I wondered. It felt exciting, that perhaps there was a scenario in which it was acceptable to break the rules.

I didn't play these videos to make myself aroused, at least not consciously. I was fascinated by them and was trying to understand what sex was all about. What kinds of positions to do (doggy, cowgirl), what kinds of noises to make (loud), what kinds of movements to try (wriggling, flinging, scratching). In the absence of both detailed sex education and honest conversations with my family or friends, these secret screenings of my mum's pornos helped me piece together what sex actually was. I already knew what sex was supposed to do (make a baby, pleasure a man), but now I knew what it was supposed to look like. Of course, it couldn't teach me what sex was supposed to *feel* like, but I didn't know yet that this was the point.

I'm not the only one who used pornography as a way of supplementing my own sex education. According to a recent report by the British Board of Film Classification (BBFC), kids often stumble across porn from as young as seven, which is often before they receive sex ed at school. And in a recent survey by BBC Three show *Porn Laid Bare*, which surveyed 18–25 year-olds, 55% of men and 34% of women said it was their main source of sex education. I don't think there's anything fundamentally wrong with teenagers having a blueprint for what sex should be before they have it, but the problem is that most of the sex we see in porn is so unrealistic. It portrays sex as a purely a physical act, without any of the accompanying feelings, communication or even consent. It's often violent and abusive, and these distressing images can leave their marks. In fact, in 2021, Grammy-winning superstar Billie Eilish, then aged 19, spoke out on *The Howard Stern Show* about how she started watching porn aged 11, which 'really destroyed' her brain. She said that it made her struggle with dating, and even gave her nightmares. I understand how Billie feels. I know, for sure, that perceiving sex in this way had a damaging effect on my early sexual experiences. Not to mention the stringent and distorted gender roles it depicts.

When I started dating Jack, I was able to stop sneaking the videos off my mum's shelves. That was a good thing, because I was consumed by fear each time I did it (which is probably why it didn't actually turn me on). Jack's porn stash was a bit different to Mum's – his videos were more modern, with better lighting and more sophisticated cameras. The women were frequently hairless, with bleached blonde hair and tiny waists. The men had scarily big dicks, which they used to penetrate the women aggressively. The storylines seemed pretty similar though; men were characterised as predators, and women as their prey. But, of course, the women seemed to enjoy this power play, willingly taking on the submissive role, and looking sexy while doing it. Romance, if there was any at all, involved dramatic and passionate kissing, with women being thrown onto beds. Forcefulness always seemed to take priority over tenderness.

I thought porn acted as a necessary guide, because I had no idea what I was doing. It taught me how to put on a good show. I flung my (long, straight, chemically relaxed) hair around, arched my back, scratched and screamed and repeated the phrases the porn stars used. I writhed around, as if my body was somehow being taken over by the women on the screen. I viewed sex like a performance, and I was in the starring role. Each time Jack finished, I felt like I deserved a standing ovation. I thought the biggest sign of 'good sex' was how well you played the role, rather than whether you actually liked it.

I know I wasn't the only one influenced by porn. Jack – and the sexual partners who came afterwards – also seemed to embody what they saw on screen. My second boyfriend told me he had a lot more experience in the bedroom than he actually did (which I wouldn't discover until later). Whenever we had sex, it was clear he was just emulating what he had seen in porn. He would pound me aggressively, as I shouted and screeched. We were both just two teenagers, pretending we knew what we were doing, and pretending to enjoy it. It's a shame, really, that we were both focused so much on giving each other the 'right' image that there was no space for vulnerability. As teenagers, inexperience is expected, and part of the joy of sex should've been exploration; gentleness, generosity and plenty of giggling as we figured out what felt good. Porn ruined that for us.

Although it felt helpful and necessary, porn also damaged my self-image. While I was trying to live up to being as sexy as the girls on screen, I knew I was always going to fall short. For starters, the women in these movies always seemed to have incredible bodies – perfect hour-glass figures with blemish-free skin, perky tits and toned bottoms. I – and pretty much every other girl I knew – did not have that body type. I had scars and stretch marks, and no matter how much I arched my back or sucked in my stomach, I would never look like the perfect porn star. There was so much I could learn from them – the right sounds and facial expressions – but there were also so many areas where I would just never match up. Plus, they were basically all white, with long blonde hair and blue eyes. All this did was reinforce what I had already been fed – that my blackness was undesirable, and that a carbon-copy image of whiteness is what men *really* find attractive. Without realising it, the absence of seeing myself in the sex I was watching impacted my self-esteem. It made me think that true sexiness was a space I'd never be able to occupy.

Over the years, my absorption of porn shifted from something I did purely for education, to a fun activity. Not fully comprehending the impact it was having on my self-esteem, I realised it could also enhance my sexual experiences. I'd go into Soho with my boyfriend to pick out porn movies from sex shops – it was exciting and fun as we picked the most raunchy plots (I always liked the ones that involved threesomes, which I later realised was a fantasy of mine). We'd watch it together, under the covers, commenting on what we liked, and what turned us on. It was an exhilarating build-up to sex, and always helped me feel hornier. I would always admit to the men I dated that I enjoyed watching porn, and this, I know, elevated me to some kind of higher level of womanhood. Most of my female friends seemed to hate the very idea of porn, so it wasn't something I discussed with them. In fact, I had one friend who had caught her boyfriend watching porn and was devastated, as if he'd been cheating. It always seemed strange to me, that the act of watching other people have sex was given a stamp of moral badness, and was something that women were expected to disapprove of.

Yet, there was a weird double standard – although hating porn, as a woman, seemed to be the 'norm', my partners loved the fact I watched it. 'You're not like other girls,' they'd say, which I would eat up, thinking it was a compliment (not realising they had literally insulted the entirety of womankind in the process). Although it was obvious the porn wasn't created for my gaze, there was always that appeal of being 'one of the boys'. Now I know that this is an impossible standard for women to live up to – to be feminine and well-behaved most of the time, but to be masculine and crude at exactly the right moments. My willingness to watch porn with my boyfriends seemed to grant me the perfect balance.

As I progressed into my twenties and thirties, my relationship with porn shifted again. The first free, advertising-supported and easily accessible porn websites first popped up in around 2006, when I was 26 years old. Suddenly, porn became so much easier to access, and there was a *lot* to choose from. Everything from anal sex, to foot fetishes, to every variety of threesome and foursome you could imagine. But the accessibility and variety didn't make me feel vindicated, free to watch whatever and whenever I pleased – in fact, it made me feel dirtier and more ashamed.

Just as I was growing into my identity as a feminist, the link between porn and patriarchy came into sharp focus. I could tell that all the porn on these sites was created through the male gaze, and marketing to those desires had distinctly misogynistic undertones. The most popular videos, with the highest numbers of hits, seemed to involve women being penetrated by multiple men from all sides, with men grabbing them or ejaculating on their faces. I couldn't understand how that could be enjoyable for a woman, but clearly it was giving the impression to men who were watching that these kinds of sexual interactions were not only normal, but desirable. A recurring theme involved very young-looking women who were enticed into having sex with their stepdads. This power dynamic grossed me out, and I hated the preoccupation with youth. Even if I tried to avoid those particular videos, it seemed that porn was becoming more and more violent. It makes sense that the more competition there was, the more porn producers felt they had to give something unexpected and exciting. Increasing numbers of unpleasant porn videos started going viral (like the infamous 'two girls, one cup', which I'd rather not recount for you but I can tell you that it involves human poo being eaten), which portrayed women's sexuality as a kind of commodity. Something to stare at; even something to laugh at.

This, I learned, was having a cataclysmic and damaging effect on modern sexuality. In 2011, a feminist researcher called Gail Dines wrote a book called *Pornland: How Porn*

Has Hijacked Our Sexuality, arguing exactly that. She suggested that the prevalence of porn had made men (who made up the majority of the viewers) desensitised to the images they were seeing. This meant they were constantly seeking out increasingly violent and aggressive imagery. She argued that this was feeding into the real world and affecting how men were acting during sex, creating a vision that sex is all about misogynistic power play rather than intimacy and exploration. She argued that these images were bad for the women watching too. In an interview with the *Guardian*, she said: 'The more porn images filter into mainstream culture, the more girls and women are stripped of full human status and reduced to sex objects. This has a terrible effect on girls' sexual identity because it robs them of their own sexual desire.'

Reading this, I reflected on my own experiences watching porn, and thought there was probably some truth to that. The porn I had seen in my youth probably did, subconsciously, make me feel like I only existed as an object, acting out desires rather than fully living them. And now, the biggest mainstream porn sites didn't feel like safe spaces for me to get aroused. It felt like they weren't created for me, and, browsing them without a partner, I was simply a dirty intruder. And even if I tried to avoid the weirdest, most demoralising videos, scrolling through the sites often meant I saw more than I bargained for, and those feelings of shame would begin to creep in.

I felt uncomfortable with so much of what I saw. First, there's the weird obsession with race. In 2021, categories like 'ebony', 'Japanese' and 'Korean' ranked among Pornhub's most-clicked categories. Seeing women from non-Caucasian ethnicities in their own 'categories', as if they were some kind of fetish, felt so dehumanising. In fact, anything that deviated outside the 'norm' of white, plastic and blonde seemed to have its own category – there are even sections called 'chubby' and 'fat'. This all just reinforces the idea that there is only one standard of beauty, and everything that falls outside that is only arousing for deviants. God forbid someone could be sexy because of who they are, and how they carry themselves, rather than possessing a very narrow set of 'acceptable' features. At the same time, the presence of these categories shows that lots of men do find these women attractive, and they're actively seeking out those videos. So, who makes the rules? Who gets to decide what the 'norm' is, and what belongs in a separate category?

Then, there's the obsession with youth: 'teen sex' remains a hugely popular search term on porn sites. And although many videos nowadays about teen sex have disclaimers on them that all the actors are over 18, it made me feel incredibly uneasy to see so many women who looked underage, and to think about the number of men getting aroused over such images. This only serves to reinforce already prevailing ideas of young girls as sex objects. It's gross, and we really need to change this mentality. Yet, it appears to me that the owners of these porn sites don't seem to care what kinds of damaging messaging they're putting across – for them, it's all about clicks, advertising and money. In 2020, a *New York Times* article exposed Pornhub's failure to take down videos depicting rape and child abuse. It's pretty disgusting.

In fact, so much of the porn industry is stained by allegations of wrongdoing and exploitation. In 2019, an NBC documentary exposed that Derek Hay, one of pornography's leading agents, had been accused by several women of 'fraud, sexual abuse, and links to an illegal escort business'. His trial is expected in 2022. And it seems like new allegations are continually coming to light, even in the wake of #MeToo. It's so disappointing.

According to Yomi Adegoke in a *Guardian* article, the porn industry is allowed to get away with repeated misdoings and allegations of sexual misconduct because any attempt to regulate it is 'deemed diametrically opposed to its need to be "dirty"', and a fear of appearing 'puritanical' prevents meaningful criticism of the industry. It's as though porn is the one place where anything goes – a space where violence, exploitation and abuse can go unchecked. And all because there's money to be made, and horny men to be satiated.

So, like many other women, I came to the conclusion that porn was inherently bad. The space wasn't created for us, and it was clear we weren't welcome (unless we were watching it alongside our male partners, being the perfect 'cool girl'). It portrayed unrealistic ideas of sex and womanhood that gave men a blueprint about what we 'should' be like (both in the bedroom and life), and this perfect woman felt impossible to live up to. And, of course, the industry itself felt so grimy and misogynistic, that watching it felt like I was somehow contributing to the exploitation. I didn't want any part of that.

Yet, I still craved the kind of titillation that only porn could provide. It was exciting and naughty; watching other people have sex could get me in the mood when I wasn't, and push me over the edge if I was. But I decided that porn simply wasn't for strong, feminist, independent women like me, so I avoided watching it as much as possible. And if I did find myself feeling horny and intrigued, logging onto a porn site, the shame and guilt would settle in my stomach, getting bigger and bigger with every hair toss and fake scream.

*

It goes without saying, porn can be fucking harmful, for both the people watching it, and the people performing in it. But just because the status quo of the porn world is problematic, doesn't mean it can't be done right. I realised this five years ago, when I discovered ethical porn that was tailored to women. I learned that porn doesn't have to be unrealistic, violent, exploitative or shameful; in fact, it can be erotic, true-to-life and sexually enhancing in a way I never imagined.

I first stumbled across Erika Lust when I was scrolling through Instagram. I read that she was a Swedish indie erotic filmmaker, who made a name for herself as one of the pioneers of feminist and ethical porn. The idea that porn could be both feminist and ethical intrigued me, as both of these claims seemed to be the antithesis of the porn world I knew. So I decided to research her, and discovered that she runs four online cinemas, XConfessions, Lust Cinema, Else Cinema and The Store by Erica Lust, all of which contain porn movies that are designed specifically through the female gaze. Rather than focusing on male pleasure and sexual athletics, they focus on the eroticism of human sexuality and relationships. To add to this, she claimed not to ever typecast performers based on age, ethnicity, sexuality or gender, and her movies represent a wide range of identities, sexualities and human body types.

Already, I was sold. The idea that I wouldn't have to stumble across another reductive 'black cock' or 'teen sex' category made my eyes light up. But then I discovered that she also follows a strict ethical code. The code includes: paying everyone fairly, from interns to performers; being transparent about who is involved in making the films; and ensuring safe sex by requiring every performer to have an STI test and choose a safe method of contraception. Each part of the film is discussed and agreed upon with all performers well before the shoot (so actors won't be surprised with some aggressive semen squirted on their face), all shoots should be created with a welcoming atmosphere (so no seedy basement sets) and every director or studio is paid a fair commission. Reading all this, I was ready to sign up.

I paid for a subscription to XConfessions and soon discovered that Erika Lust's porn films were game-changing. Not only are they beautifully shot – so much more cinematic and aesthetically pleasing than any other porn film I had watched – they did exactly as they promised; featured women of all different races, shapes and sizes. These women were all desiring and being desired. Finally, I felt like I could see myself (and other women I knew) represented in sexy scenes. It helped me believe that I could be the object of desire and eroticism. Also, the films made me fucking horny. Although, at first, it took me a little while to get my head round this new and enlightening kind of video.

Seeing as Erika Lust's porn completely transformed the way I consumed it, I was keen to speak to her about what led her to starting ethical porn. She told me that, like me, she had felt uncomfortable with the porn she watched as a teenager. 'I felt conflicted – those videos I saw got me aroused somehow, but at the same time, it wasn't really pleasurable as I felt that something was wrong with them, both ethically, and in terms of content,' she said. 'It was also clear that those videos weren't created with female viewers in mind. When you're a teenager, it's easy to come to the conclusion that something is wrong with you, and that porn just isn't for you as a woman.'

When she was studying at university in Sweden, she came across Linda Williams's book, *Hard Core*, and she had a 'eureka moment' about porn: 'I realised that most stereo-typical porn is not something that reflects the truth about sex – it's a statement that expresses ideologies, values and opinions about sex and gender.'

After her studies she moved to Barcelona, where she started taking film classes, which is where she decided to create her own adult film, one that would express her values and show the importance of female pleasure. Her short film, *The Good Girl*, went viral. 'Soon I began to receive letters from people all over the world telling me that they loved the film and asked when I'd be making more,' she explained. 'I realised that there were more people out there who wanted an alternative pornography and I was presented with an opportunity to help change the land-scape of the industry, and so Erika Lust Films was born.'

I love the fact that her sites contain an abundance of different plots and storylines. Just because the porn is made with the female gaze in mind doesn't mean that all women want is romance, stroking and kissing. In fact, women often want the grabbing and fucking type of porn too – and you can also find plenty of that. 'We can't gener-alise our desires as every woman is obviously different,' Erika explained. 'But I think what really excites and empowers women is to have a voice in the story, both on screen and in real life. Women want to see other women enjoying and freely living their sexuality while they are in charge of their bodies, whether the film is romantic, kinky or anything in-between.'

And my favourite part is that, for every porn movie, there are interviews with the actors and directors, where they talk about who they are, and answer some questions about the movie. There's something so satisfying about that. Rather than destroying the fantasy image of the sex, remembering that these people are real-life humans rather than just sexual objects actually made the sex seem *more* enjoyable. Somehow, Erika's movies allowed me to explore that one aspect of sex that I thought porn would never be able to help with – the feelings behind it. But by creating sex that is realistic and, fundamentally, human, I could be fully immersed in what was happening and allow my pleas-ure to take over.

For Erika, this part of the process is also really important for humanising the people who work in an industry that is so heavily stigmatised. 'Interviews and behind-the-scenes are so important to me as they give a feel of what sex performing is really about, and what the ideals, dreams and beliefs are of the sex workers and erotic directors,' she said. 'We need to normalise sex work as real work, and put an end to stigma, criminalisation and dehumanisation.'

Discovering Erika's porn catalogue made me feel like I was finally vindicated in enjoying porn. Clearly, the popularity of her films shows that there are hundreds of thousands of women out there who feel exactly as I do – they want the arousal and fantasy that porn provides, without all the uncomfortable feelings and misogyny. Rather than believing porn must be intrinsically bad and shameful, I realised that porn actually *does* have its benefits. In fact, one study by psychologist Sean McNabney looked at how porn consumption affects women's satisfaction and relationships. He found that more frequent porn-use was related to less difficulty in becoming aroused, and greater orgasm pleasure, both alone and during partnered sex.

Rather than being forbidden and shameful, it turns out that porn can be a healthy and enhancing aspect of our sex lives. 'Porn provides a safe space to learn new things, explore fantasies, and have parts of your identity validated,' wrote educator Ruby Rare in her book, *Sex Ed*. 'It can allow you to dive into the broadest variety of sexual fantasies imaginable.'

Plus, there's nothing to be ashamed of when exploring desires through porn. You might watch porn videos that feature actors doing something you wouldn't really want to try in real life – like choking, or perhaps orgies – and porn can be a safe space to explore these fantasies. We need to stop seeing our porn preferences as somehow wrapped up in who we are and what we like – often, what gets us aroused can be completely different to our real-life preferences. And that's totally okay.

'Fantasy and reality are different,' Dr Laurie Mintz, sexuality psychologist and author of *Becoming Cliterate*, told me. 'If you get turned on by violent porn, it doesn't mean you want violent sex. Part of it is just being a little more accepting of yourself rather than worrying what's wrong with you. Give yourself permission to enjoy what you enjoy as long as it's consensual.'

In recent years, I've felt more empowered to open up about enjoying porn with female friends. I've recommended Erika Lust's films to more people than I can count, and I love that so many of them have told me they've enjoyed them. Often, this is the first time they've ever liked watching porn. There's absolutely no shame in enjoying something that men also enjoy. Women are sexual beings too, with fantasies and desires to match any man's, and I'm pleased that the mainstream porn industry is beginning to see that. The proportion of female visitors on Pornhub has been growing steadily, and in 2021, women made up 31% of the viewers in the UK. Categories like 'porn for women' are garnering even more clicks, and there are plenty more platforms popping up that offer porn for the female gaze.

Clearly, though, Erika is leading the way in the ethical porn space – and the entire industry needs to follow her lead. 'The porn industry's highest positions of power are still overwhelmingly dominated by white cisgender men,' she told me. 'In male-directed, heterosexual porn, the female becomes the object of the combined gaze of the filmmaker, male performer and male viewer – so the women always become secondary. This is why I believe that in order for porn to change, we need more women, queer, BIPOC, Asian people behind the cameras. The most crucial difference between my indie porn and a massive amount of mainstream porn is that I constantly show my name, face and share my values with the public.'

We also need to normalise paying for our porn. Before, I would've been ashamed to admit I'd taken out a paid subscription with a porn site, but now I'm proud that I'm contributing to an ethical industry where workers are paid fairly. 'When you pay for porn, you are giving it value,' Erika agreed. 'That's why, if you want it to change, you need to start paying for it in the same way you would for Netflix or Spotify. When you pay for porn, you are supporting the people who do it, and you're sending a message that you want to watch porn that is made safely, with quality and diversity, acknowledging that sex work is work.'

According to Ruby Rare, we should all be expanding our idea of what porn actually means. Rather than watching a porn video, you might find that erotic fiction (think *Fifty Shades of Grey*, or even some fan fiction on Wattpad) is the perfect way to get yourself tingling. Or perhaps you'd prefer erotic storytelling through audiobooks and podcasts; if so, the website Dipsea is perfect. There are hundreds of sexy stories you can tune into, close your eyes and imagine for yourself. Creating the visions in your head means they're perfectly tailored to you. For me, Erika Lust's porn films are my favourite. I watch them alone, with a glass of wine in bed, and sometimes I'll watch them with a partner too. I love that they can make me feel like myself, sexually, when I'm on my own, but that they can also act as a bonding experience when I'm with someone else. Either way, I don't feel any shame and I'm open about how enhancing they are for me.

I even speak to my children about watching porn. I want them to know what it is, before they stumble across it (like I did) and feel ashamed and confused by what they are seeing. I've tried to prepare them for the lack of realism they'll start seeing in porn in their teen years, which I hope will take the power out of it. I never want them to feel insecure because of what they've seen. Like so many conversations about sex, I know it's hard for parents to admit to watching porn. It's easier to just ignore the problem and hope they don't see any of the bad shit. But it's just not reality. Preparing children for what porn is – and explaining that, often, it is not representative of real sex – is so important.

I have come on quite a journey with how I view porn. In my teen years, it was primarily an educational resource; a guiding light for what I 'should' be doing, and what I 'should' look like. But as I tried to bend myself into their impossible sex positions, and held myself up against their impossible beauty standards, I found that porn was affecting me as it affects so many other women; bruising my self-esteem, making me feel unsexy and inadequate. In my twenties, the explosion of online porn solidified the negative image I had, and I criticised its lack of realism, and lack of ethics. Now, though, I've found the right porn for me, and I truly believe it elevates my sex life. It makes me feel liberated and goddess-like, and most importantly, it's *fun* to watch. We all love watching movies, but being able to watch a film that offers you the opportunity to orgasm (during or after) – who wouldn't want that?

My biggest hope is that, eventually, the entire mainstream porn industry will follow ethical standards. I hope that, in the near future, all porn stars are treated with dignity and respect, so that the industry can be a truly safe space for desires and fantasies to be met. I hope that men will watch porn and not believe they have to perform aggressively to impress women; I hope they will see realistic porn that places vulnerability and communication above heavy thrusting and unrealistic orgasm noises. I hope that all women and non-binary people will see themselves in the porn they watch, that it can boost their confidence rather than making them feel inadequate. I hope you, dear reader, will discover porn that will allow you to explore your wildest desires, to liberate you sexually and remind you that you are completely normal, and your pleasure is worthy and valid. There's a reason porn exists – to titillate, excite, arouse – and we all deserve the chance to get in on the action.

What I've learned about porn:

- Watching porn to get you off isn't bad or shameful. But the best approach is to seek out feminist, ethical porn that is made by women, like Erika Lust's sites. Other great ethical sites include MakeLoveNotPorn and PinkLabel.

- We have to remember what porn is good for (titillation and arousal) and what it's not good for: education. Even ethical porn is stylised, so I don't think porn should ever be used as a means of learning about real sex between real people. We need to have much more interactive, open discussions about sex, so that porn isn't misused for educational purposes.

- Paying for porn is the only way you can guarantee that what you're watching is ethically made. Signing up for a membership isn't a waste of money, and it's also nothing to be ashamed of.

- Find the kind of porn that's right for you – if you like romantic storylines, that's great. If you prefer rough sex, find ethical porn that portrays this in a safe and consensual way. Listen to sexy audiobooks, or read erotic fiction. Go for whatever makes you horny.

4

Orgasms

ORGASM (noun): the climax of sexual excitement, characterised by intensely pleasurable feelings centred in the genitals and (in men) experienced as an accompaniment to ejaculation.

For me, having an orgasm is on par with meditating. When I reach climax, I feel completely at one with myself. I'm no longer focusing on external realities; my mind goes blank and the sensation in my body takes over. For a few seconds, nothing else matters – not my next Instagram post, not what I'm cooking my kids for dinner, not paying my bills. Everything else fades away and, for a few exquisite moments, it's just me, my body and my pleasure. Not to be dramatic, but I honestly think having an orgasm connects me to a higher power. Once it's over, I feel ever-so-slightly transformed; satisfied and calmed. I'm the kind of person who finds it difficult to clear my mind, but orgasm is one of the only times where I feel fully present.

But orgasming hasn't always felt like such a spiritual experience. For much of my life, orgasms have felt elusive, confusing and impossible to achieve. I struggled to orgasm for many years; throughout my twenties, it happened rarely and I never knew why or how it occurred to try to make it happen again. Because of this, I felt like there was something profoundly wrong with me. The women in movies and porn seemed to orgasm every time they had sex (often at the same time as their male partner) and it seemed so easy, so effortless. I felt like I was chasing a high that was out of reach. My inability to reach hair-tossing, open-mouthed, earth-shattering orgasms within a few thrusts of penetrative sex made me feel like I was failing as a woman.

Like so many parts of my sexual journey, I know that the problem originates with the lack of information I had about orgasms growing up – and the shame we all had around talking openly and honestly about it. From everything I had seen, I could tell that women were supposed to have some kind of body-shuddering experience during sex, but there was a complete black hole of information about what that actually was, and what it was supposed to feel like in practice.

When I was 12, one of my friends told me (in typical bragging teenager fashion) that her boyfriend made her orgasm all the time.

At that point, I thought 'orgasm' was just another fancy word for male ejaculation. So hearing that there was a female orgasm was intriguing; it seemed like a mythical creature, as rare and magical as a unicorn. Amazed and curious, I asked: 'What does it feel like?'

'Just amazing!' she said dramatically, with a smirk and a hair toss.

Not satisfied with her answer, I asked, 'But what does it actually feel like?'

She paused to consider my question, before responding, matter-of-factly: 'It's a bit like needing to pee.'

This seemed very odd to me. I didn't understand how the feeling of needing to pee could be pleasurable; needing the loo didn't feel like a sexual experience. Plus, I was worried that having an orgasm would mean wetting myself, which seemed like it would be embarrassing. Despite all that, I was determined to know what it felt like.

I can't pinpoint the first time I had an orgasm. I think it's because I didn't know how to identify it; besides my friend's (incredibly oversimplified) description, and the images I had seen in porn, I had no idea what I was supposed to be looking for. But I do know that, with my college boyfriend (who would eventually become my husband), I would often experience pleasure that would simmer and build until I'd feel like I was sinking into a warm puddle of liquid gold. But was that an orgasm? I didn't know. I thought orgasms involved some kind of huge explosion. It felt great, but it didn't make me scream and shout and rip the bedsheets apart with my nails, like the women I had seen on screen. I only let out a whimper, really. It also didn't really feel like needing a wee, and I definitely didn't wet myself. I had seen the porn movies where women looked like they were ejaculating, and I had heard male friends and boyfriends talk about how amazingly sexy this kind of 'squirting' was. I had no idea what the liquid was, or whether orgasm only counted if you managed it. But I did know that I had never done it, and that made me feel shit about myself. Without having the right information about what was 'normal', I didn't know whether the sensations I was feeling were orgasms at all.

To add to the confusion, these intense pleasurable feelings only ever happened during 'foreplay' – when I was being fingered or licked out (I wouldn't discover that I could actually touch my own body during sex until later). It was always when my clitoris was being stimulated. It certainly never happened during penetrative sex alone. I found that, a lot of the time, fingers or tongues could be more pleasurable than a thrusting penis, but I was far too shy to admit that.

That's because there was (and still is) a dominant idea that a 'vaginal orgasm' (i.e. caused by penetration alone) is the most important kind. Sigmund Freud said that, while women often experienced pleasure from stimulation of the clitoris, the vaginal orgasm was superior and more mature. His theories were focused around married, heterosexual intercourse, and women who couldn't orgasm in this way were often described as 'frigid' or assumed to be lesbians – which was considered to be a mental illness at the time. Orgasms were just one more way of stigmatising women; for making them feel guilty for sitting outside the narrow confines of 'ideal' womanhood.

Even though Freud was speaking from the early twentieth century, his ideas clearly lived on, as I felt this stigma too. I thought that I should be achieving the most amazing, mind-blowing orgasms from the friction of a moving penis, but it just didn't seem to work that way for me. So I internalised the idea that I was somehow abnormal. Either I lacked the sensation receptors that other women had, or, perhaps more worryingly, there was something dysfunctional about me as a person. Either way, it didn't feel good.

It didn't help that everyone was obsessed with the idea of the G-spot. According to friends and magazines, locating and stimulating your G-spot was the secret behind achieving the highly coveted vaginal orgasm. American researcher Dr Beverly Whipple first published the term 'G-spot' in 1981, when she suggested that you can find it by making a 'come here' motion with your finger on the inside of your vagina. If you could angle it right, and stimulate this spot, you could apparently have those porn-worthy orgasms I was desperate to discover. I remember, once, asking a boyfriend to touch me like that, to see if we could figure it out. I knew there were some parts of my vagina that felt more sensitive than others, for sure, and I wanted to explore new sensations, but he wasn't so keen. It left me feeling even more frustrated and confused, and more like a failure, than I did before.

So without the ability to make it, I had no choice but to fake it. Throughout my twenties, I faked an orgasm pretty much every time I had sex. Don't get me wrong – it's not that I outright lied, and said I had orgasmed. It's just that I knew to increase the pace of my breathing, make guttural moaning sounds and contort my body so that it looked like I was having one. I always did this when I was ready for sex to end, because I knew that giving the impression of orgasm would make my partner come quicker, so that I could get back to watching my TV show, or doing literally anything else that felt more exciting than penetrative sex. It sounds brutal, but sometimes sex felt like a chore, like something I had to do, and initiate, in order to keep a relationship going and 'healthy.' So if faking intense pleasure meant I'd get to the finishing line quicker, it was a no-brainer to do it.

I'm not alone in this. It's incredibly normal for women in heterosexual relationships to fake orgasms regularly. A 2019 study found that almost 59% of women said they had faked orgasms. And their reasons were pretty similar to mine; of those, 44.6% said they did it to bring sex to an end. The study also found that the most common reason women fake orgasms is because they want to make their partner feel more successful (57%), with 37.7% of the women also saying they liked their partner and didn't want them to feel bad. I know that these reasons definitely played a role in my consistent fakery too. It brings us back to the idea that sex is completely based around the man's pleasure, and that the very act of sex is a power play where men must come out victorious. I think women fake orgasms because we've been trained to stroke very fragile male egos. We believe that if we don't make them feel masculine – able to satisfy a woman through the sole power of their magical penis – then this could backfire on us, somehow. Girls are trained from a young age to keep everyone happy and not to rock the boat, and this mentality plays out in sex too. Pretending you've had an orgasm is just an easy way to ensure no one's feelings are hurt. It's that 'good girl' mentality creeping in again; the idea that the perfect woman must place everyone else's feelings above her own.

Orgasms

My inability to orgasm – at least in the way I deemed to be 'normal' or acceptable – was not something I talked about with my friends, or even my boyfriends. Instead, it was a shame I buried deep inside. Revealing it would be like admitting I was broken. I didn't want to make it known that sex left me feeling constantly disappointed. Of course, I loved the physical intimacy, I got a buzz off seeing my partner enjoy himself and be turned on by me, and I definitely did experience waves of pleasure and sensation. But the deep-rooted belief that there was something fundamentally wrong with me held me back from enjoying sex as much as I could have.

*

As it happens, I'm not as abnormal as I always believed. Research suggests that only around 18% of women can reach orgasm through penetrative sex alone, and, when I asked my followers on Instagram, 36% of you said you find it difficult to orgasm. These numbers are astoundingly high given the over-representation of the female orgasm through penetrative sex in both porn and mainstream movies. So why do real-life women find it so hard? Well, it's partly down to the misguided idea that women should feel the most pleasure inside the vagina – when really, the clitoris is where it's all happening. It's the most sensitive erogenous zone on the female body, as it's packed with around 8,000 nerve endings that, when stimulated, elicit a strong sexual physiological response. For context, the male penis contains around 4,000 nerve endings. With that in mind, you realise it's pretty fucking powerful. In the 1960s, William Masters and Virginia Johnson, the ground-breaking sex researchers (who you might know from the TV drama, *Masters of Sex*), actually debunked Freud's idea that the 'vaginal' orgasm was a more 'mature' orgasm; they found that the physiology of the orgasm response was identical whether stimulation was clitoral or vaginal. That was several decades ago, but I suppose deep-rooted beliefs can take a while to unlearn.

More in-depth studies into female anatomy have shown that the hyper-sensitive part, just above the vagina, is only the external part of the clitoris – the tip of the iceberg, if you will. The organ itself is actually much bigger.

'The whole structure of the clitoris is around about 9cm long and 6cm wide, with most of it hidden under the skin,' Dr Karen Gurney told me. 'It's equivalent in structure and function to the penis, meaning it fills with blood on arousal just like the penis does.'

So, Dr Gurney explained, 'vaginal orgasms' are not necessarily caused by a specific 'G-spot', but just the hidden parts of the clitoris. 'The G-spot basically refers to where the clitoris wraps around the vagina, and it's a sensitive area on the front wall. Some people notice it, but not everyone does.' In fact, she explained, we all experience pleasure at slightly different points, depending on our anatomy. For most women and people with vulvas, though, the most sensitive part is that little pea-sized tip, right at the top – and not, in fact, inside the vaginal wall at all.

It was reassuring to discover that I'm not weird or abnormal for often finding 'foreplay' – the parts where I experienced external stimulation – to be more rewarding than penetrative sex. But it also made me realise that describing sexual acts like mutual masturbation and oral sex as 'foreplay' is fucking problematic. In fact, this is something that sex experts like Dr Laurie Mintz are hoping to address. In her book, *Becoming Cliterate*, Mintz explains that the word 'foreplay' assumes these sexual acts are the 'appetiser, rather than the main meal'. Again, this places men at the centre of sexual gravity – it assumes that all sexual acts leading up to their ejaculation are simply the starters. It's even more problematic because it's such a heteronormative idea. When women are intimate with each other, the main ways they 'have sex' involve oral and hand stimulation. And guess what? They have more orgasms than women in heterosexual relationships. Research suggests that 65% of heterosexual women 'usually' orgasm during sexual activity, but for women who have sex with women, the number leaps up to 86%.

So what does this show us? Beyond the fact that women probably know women's bodies better than men do (shock), it's further evidence that placing emphasis on what is usually considered 'foreplay' actually reaps far more orgasmic reward. Expanding our definition of what counts as 'sex' can be extremely beneficial for women's pleasure, especially because many women struggle with pain during penetrative sex. And I'm sure it's not just women who enjoy the touchy-feely mouthy stuff – I can imagine plenty of men favour blow jobs over penetrative sex. Not to mention, people of both sexes actually become wild with arousal from the idea of pleasuring their partners in this way. We really need to start giving other forms of erotic intimacy the credit they deserve. Touching can be the main meal rather than just the starter. It can be incredibly beautiful, powerful – and orgasm-inducing.

But the persistent emphasis on penetrative sex explains why there's such difference between the way men and women in heterosexual relationships experience pleasure. Research suggests that 95% of men 'usually' orgasm during sex with women – that's a whopping 30% more than their female partners. This difference is often referred to as the 'orgasm gap'. Like the pay gap, experts insist that this imbalance is not due to any biological reasons – Dr Karen Gurney, author of *Mind The Gap*, points out that the rates of how often women have orgasms alone, or with other women, tell us that women have a similar orgasmic capacity to men. But like the pay gap, it's a reflection of patriarchal and misogynistic attitudes towards sex.

'The underlying reason for the orgasm gap is the overvaluing and privileging of male sexual pleasure and the devaluing of female sex pleasure,' Dr Laurie Mintz told me when we spoke. It's even noticeable in the culturally ingrained language we use. 'We call our entire genitals a "vagina", which is one part – the canal where penises go in and babies come out,' Dr Mintz said. 'By doing that, we're linguistically erasing the clitoris, and calling our genitals by the part that is more sexually responsive to men than women themselves. We use the words "sex" and "intercourse" as if they're one and the same. That language perpetuates the idea of sex as a means of bringing men to orgasm, not women.'

Orgasms

Why? Well, we can't ignore the fact that the male orgasm serves a very specific function in society – to make babies. But, of course, this isn't the same for women; we don't need to orgasm to get pregnant. For years, scientists have tried to uncover why women even have orgasmic capabilities at all. Some studies have suggested that climaxing served a purpose in the more primitive version of our species, as it aided ovulation. The evidence is a little hazy, but there's also the more convincing argument that orgasms make women want to have sex more, therefore increasing the chance of reproduction and serving an evolutionary purpose. Either way, though, societies all over the world have long decided that female pleasure is unnecessary and unimportant at best. At worst, it has been viewed as a sign of raging witchy female hysteria. Living a life filled with pleasure was something men could do freely, in contrast to the angelic baby-making servants women were expected to be. To have urges, to want more ... well, it simply wasn't allowed. And, sadly, these age-old ideas still linger today.

Prioritising male pleasure is so entwined with the whole act of heterosexual sex. It's so ingrained for us to perceive male ejaculation as the 'end' of sex; the final explosion of confetti at the finishing line. Any pleasure we might receive before then is a bonus, not the end-goal. After my partner would come, I'd never feel like I could ask for him to do anything more. That was sex done, over; he'd collapse onto the bed with a grin on his face, we'd turn our backs to each other and fall asleep. I felt like I'd done my job. I would never reveal to him – or even, I think, to myself – that I had more wants and needs that hadn't been fulfilled. Now, I realise that those feelings of disappointment and dissatisfaction stem from not knowing I was allowed to ask.

With the policing of female desire, and the lack of emphasis placed on our sexual pleasure, it's unsurprising that women harbour so much shame about our roles as sexual beings. There's a massive contradiction: we feel guilty about wanting to orgasm, but we also feel pressure for not being able to. And if you mix both of these conflicting feelings together, what do you get? Probably the worst conditions ever to be able to orgasm.

The more I've worried about not being able to orgasm, the harder it's become. As I mentioned before, orgasms can be like meditation – they offer a chance to tune out from the world and become at one with your body. But when I'm constantly thinking about other things – including the fact I'm taking ages to orgasm, what food is in the fridge, and what my schedule looks like tomorrow – I find it incredibly difficult to let go. My body can't enter that state of orgasmic meditation, because my brain simply won't let it. Emptying my mind can be challenging. Often, it's bombarded with intrusive thoughts just as the pleasure begins to build. And when I posted on my Instagram about this, I learned that plenty of my followers feel the same way. Lots of them said they're often held back from orgasms because distracting thoughts get in the way. They cited anxiety, stress and worries as the biggest roadblocks.

According to Dr Karen Gurney, this is all very normal. 'Physical touch, in terms of what someone else is doing to your body, is only a third of the picture when it comes to the ability to have an orgasm during partnered sex,' Dr Gurney explained. 'The other parts are about how turned on you are, what's going on in your head, and how closely the situation matches your optimal conditions for good sex. So, how do you feel about the other person? How turned on are you? How hot is the position you're in – what can you see, and is that erotic for you? The last bit of the puzzle is what you're thinking about, so if you're easily distracted or struggle with attention anyway, this reduces your sexual arousal, reduces the pleasure you feel and can get in the way of orgasm. And, frustratingly, worrying about orgasm operates in that way as well. The more focused you are on "am I going to come?", the less focused you are on what is happening sexually.'

Because of this, I truly believe that orgasms are less about you or your partner's actions, and more about how you're feeling inside. I'm pretty sure I could have the best, most attractive lover in the world with their head between my legs, but if I was feeling stressed, unconfident or out of sorts, I still wouldn't be able to come.

It can also be difficult to tune into the pleasure in your body when you're constantly trying to see yourself through the eyes of your partner. Having viewed sex as a perform- ance for much of my life, I've often spent sex focusing on how I'm looking. Am I making sexy facial expressions? Do my boobs look good? I know that focusing all my attention on how I was being perceived stopped me from being fully present. The more we focus our energy outward, on pleas- ing others, it becomes increasingly difficult to focus inward, to please ourselves.

*

So, orgasms can be hard to achieve. Everything about the female orgasm is shrouded in confusion, misinformation, shame, pressure and patriarchy. But, they're also magical, spiritual and fucking incredible. It took me a long time to realise that.

My relationship with orgasms started to change once I'd had my first daughter, in my thirties. Having a girl galvanised me to increase my awareness about myself. I had this overwhelming urge to understand myself and my body more. I think it's because motherhood meant I felt like more of an adult, and I started to question all my pre-existing beliefs and realised I had autonomy over my own body. At the same time, I was becoming more active on social media. I started being introduced to the idea of sex-positivity on Instagram, which opened up a whole new world of information, helping me to embrace the idea that my pleasure mattered. I started reading more about orgasms, to demystify why it wasn't happening for me, which reassured me that I was, in fact, normal. This in itself was game-changing – it really helped me to relax.

The first thing I learned was that I finally needed to get comfortable with exploring my own body. I realised I couldn't expect my partner to understand how to pleasure me if I didn't even know how to pleasure myself. It was good timing too; I hated how my post-pregnancy body looked, so I was struggling to be sexually intimate with my husband. This meant it was the perfect time to prioritise self-exploration, so I started masturbating; first with my hands, and later on with sex toys. I know, it took me until my thirties to realise I could touch my own body. Wild, right? But I'll go into my body-hatred, and my adventures in masturbation, in the next two chapters. The relationships we have with our bodies, and the stigma surrounding masturbation, are both topics that are shrouded in shame, and they deserve a lot more discussion.

But what I will say, for now, is that masturbation helped me realise that those simmering feelings of pleasure *were* in fact orgasms. Once I gave them the attention they deserved, I got to enjoy them so much more. Through trying lots of different angles, approaches and toys, I also discovered more explosive orgasms that I would feel in my whole body. I actually started experiencing something a bit more similar to the porn-worthy orgasms I had imagined. Although, for me, they didn't come from penetrative sex. I learned that there's no one singular way of coming. Some orgasms shake your whole body, some make you shout, while others build slowly and then peter out. I've learned that different methods tend to result in different orgasms (hands and sex toys can be slightly different) but even then, no two orgasms are the same. They always feel slightly different and that, I think, is part of the fun. You never know what pleasurable prize you might unwrap.

Learning how to orgasm on my own gave me the language – and the confidence – to ask for what I wanted during partnered sex. I gradually came to understand that there was no shame in needing a little something extra during penetration – whether with fingers, or sex toys like bullet vibrators – and combining clit action with penetration was beyond transformative. Not only did I begin to enjoy sex so much more, I know my partner loved it too. I think, often, we don't give our partners the credit they deserve. Especially in loving and committed relationships, we should assume that our partners actually *want* us to have a good time. They're constantly searching for clues to give us pleasure, and if we're faking noises or performing, how will they ever get the hint? It only leads to more confusion and crossed wires. If we're honest and upfront about what we want, the benefits double up – we'll have a better time, and they can feel the genuine satisfaction and happiness of seeing us in our element. If we want to make our partners believe they're great in bed, we absolutely need to stop faking it. The best possible gift we can give during sex is not an attentive blow job, but being honest and open. It's saying 'more of that', or 'a bit to the right'. Self-assuredness is far sexier than any fake moan.

And, Dr Laurie Mintz advised me, it's so important to have conversations about sex outside of the bedroom. 'No problem, including a sexual problem, can be solved without talking about it,' she said. 'I always joke with clients and say, "I promise you it's a lot easier to talk about sex than it is to learn to read your partner's mind."' And, she said, all sex therapists would suggest having the most important conversations outside of the bedroom, on neutral ground.

But how can you broach the topic, without worrying about hurting your partner's feelings? 'A good way is to say, "I was reading this book or listening to this super cool podcast and what I learned is that the overwhelming majority of women need clitoral stimulation to orgasm or their orgasms are greatly enhanced and, hey that sounds cool, I would like to do more things that focus on my clitoris, I would like to bring a vibrator", something like that.' (I fully consent to you using this book as your jumping-off board).

'You can also do some reading or watch educational things together. There's a site called omgyes.com that is great for that. Look at it as an adventure to learn together,' she suggested.

Even as a confident, well-adjusted, independent woman, you might struggle to use your voice. This happens in everyday life, all the time. And it's not something for us to beat ourselves up over – we've been conditioned to silence our own opinions and desires throughout years and years of patriarchal oppression. But our voices *do* matter, especially when it comes to sex. If you need constant snogging, or a finger in the bum, or your nipples being pinched, in order to come – it's not only okay, it's absolutely your right to ask for it. You're not weird, or demanding, or hysterical. You're just a human, with sexual desire and immense capacity to feel pleasure. And you deserve to feel what your body has given you. Put your shyness aside and start to get brave and ask for exactly what you want. If you don't know what it is that you want, start to become curious – we can only learn and grow by trying new things. It will revolutionise your sexual pleasure by getting busy with being curious.

After all, orgasms are beneficial in so many ways. First, when we orgasm, we release substantial amounts of oxytocin, a peptide hormone and neuropeptide also known as the 'cuddle hormone', which encourages social and personal bonding. So when we orgasm alone, it can encourage a deep feeling of love and satisfaction within ourselves, but when we orgasm with a partner, it can even strengthen that bond. Oxytocin helps to lower levels of cortisol, the stress hormone, which itself is linked to a variety of ailments including high blood pressure. There are even studies that suggest orgasms can be an effective form of pain relief (due to the endorphins and oxytocin), and can boost immunity. It seems that the female orgasm does serve some pretty important purposes after all.

I want this book to feel helpful; I want you to go away feeling empowered to explore your own sexual desires. But I won't give you any specific advice about how to orgasm. I know that when I've read advice in magazines or online about what finger movement or toy to use to have the best orgasms, it ends up having the reverse effect. I put too much pressure on myself and then feel ashamed or confused when it doesn't work out. The truth is, there's no one foolproof way to orgasm. What gets me off probably won't get you off, or vice versa, and we need to normalise that. Rather than following a narrow set of instructions, we need to embrace the idea of exploration and trying lots of new things. Sometimes, something will work one time, and then never happen again. It doesn't just depend on who you are; it depends on what day of the week it is, and how you're feeling in your own body. That uncertainty can seem scary, but I also think it's really fucking exciting. Exploring different techniques, moves, toys and sexual positions can be a fun adventure.

Sometimes you'll reach an orgasm, and sometimes you won't, but that's okay too. After all, I do think sex can still be pleasurable, intimate and exciting without having an orgasm, if you tune into the sensation and stimulation in a mindful way. This idea is even emphasised in the Kama Sutra, the legendary ancient Indian guide to sexuality, eroticism and fulfilment, which focuses on curiosity and pleasure. Although I do strongly believe all women deserve the joy of orgasms, it's also really important to remember that they aren't the be-all and end-all of good sex. Once we take pressure out of the equation, sex becomes so much freer – and much more fun. Focus on the journey not the destination.

Now, I can usually come when I want to – but I have to be completely relaxed. If I'm on my own, I sometimes watch porn, which helps, but even when I'm having partnered sex, I often fantasise inside my head. I'm a firm believer in removing the shame around fantasising. Just because you're having sex with your partner doesn't mean you can't envision a raunchy orgy or pretend it's your favourite actor between your legs. I used to carry a lot of internalised shame about my fantasies, but now I know that my thoughts are exactly that – *mine*. No one can police them, and there's absolutely nothing wrong with picturing an arousing scene in your head that differs from the one you're currently in. If anything, I think it helps me to become more present, as it gives me something to focus on and blocks out those frustrating intrusive thoughts.

Sometimes, though, I can't control the intrusive thoughts. If I'm feeling sad or annoyed, or I'm overwhelmingly busy, I can't switch my mind off. In these moments, I don't chastise myself. I tell myself that it's okay and I'll try again later, or even another day. We will all go through periods of having more desire and less desire; more orgasms and fewer orgasms. It's normal. It helps to remind myself that, when I'm out of my sexual groove, it will come back – I just need to give myself time, forgiveness, and a lot of love.

If you take anything away from this chapter, I want it to be this: your pleasure is worthy and valid. Whether you can have multiple orgasms a day, or you've still not experienced one yet. Whether you have full-bodied, shuddering orgasms from penetrative sex alone, or whether you need a very specific angle of tongue action for a solid 20 minutes. Whether you have your best orgasms while you're tied up and being spanked, or when you're alone with your imagination. Whatever gets you off, as long as it's not hurting anyone else, is fucking great. The strength and capacity of the female orgasm shows that our bodies are built to feel pleasure, even if the way we experience that pleasure differs. Despite the fact society has repeatedly told us we're not sexual beings, that desire isn't 'for' us, our physiology tells a completely different story. What's the point in having a clitoris if we don't utilise it whenever we fucking please?

We have so much more power than we think we do. I think that applies to every part of life, but it's important to reiterate here. Not only do we have the power to have incredible sexual pleasure, we also have the power to ask for it. Our orgasms have the capacity to be even more powerful than any man's, so they deserve at least as much attention – even if they don't include a thrusting penis. Wanting sex to involve not solely a dick but also touching, licking, stroking and vibrating (or even no dick at all) is absolutely nothing to be ashamed of. In fact, it's completely normal. I think it's only when we collectively make peace with this fact that the 'orgasm gap' will become a relic of the past. I hope that one day, women's pleasure and joy will be viewed as the valuable, spiritual and sacred thing that it is. How we feel about ourselves ultimately impacts the world around us; the more joy we experience in our bodies, the more joy we'll be able to channel into our work, our relationships, our families. Honestly, I believe that once we remove the pressure and shame surrounding female orgasms, the world will be a better place.

What I've learned about having great orgasms:

- Orgasms are bloody lovely, but they are not everything. I try to be conscious of indulging and enjoying the build-up. It's easy to be goal-oriented and miss out on the beauty in the process. In the end, this actually helps me reach orgasm easier because it takes the pressure off. Practise being fully aware of the feelings and sensations, rather than getting to the end. Taking time to be fully present is wonderful.

- There are many ways to pleasure yourself, or be pleasured, that don't necessarily have to involve genital stimulation. Try things like nipple stimulation or even neck kissing, licking, nibbling. Do a body scan and explore other parts of the body and notice the sensations.

Feeling Myself

- When we think of sex toys, we often think of those we use to masturbate, but experiment with using sex toys during partnered sex too. Whether it's placing a vibrator against your clitoris during penetration, or using an anal toy (with plenty of lube) at the same time, this could be a way to achieve orgasm with another person if you often struggle. My favourite brands of sex toy are LELO and Smile Makers.

- Get to know your own body, and then use that information to tell your partner about what you need in order to come. We can't expect our partners to know their way around our bodies automatically; we're all different, so we need to give them some guidance. Far from ruining the mood, being direct about what you want is actually really fucking sexy.

5

Bodies

A few days after giving birth to my first daughter, fresh out of the bath, I unwrapped my towel to get dressed. I stopped to stare at my naked reflection in my mirrored wardrobes. My body looked completely different to the one I'd always known. This wasn't the body I'd shown off on big nights out. It wasn't the body I'd taken travelling around Australia and Asia in my twenties, wearing bikinis and little else. It didn't even seem like the same body I had used to conceive my child. It looked like I'd been blown up with an air pump; everything was swollen, or saggy and sore. My stretch marks were red and angry. I thought I was hideous, and tears began to stream down my face. At that moment, I made a vow to never wear a bikini again, or to show too much skin in public. I truly believed everyone would be disgusted by what they saw. I felt ashamed of what I looked like and who I'd become.

I have a sneaking suspicion you've had a moment like this too. Where you looked at your own body and felt angry, sad, humiliated. Where your body felt like an enemy, and not an intimate friend you've carried your whole life. I'm assuming this because we live in a culture that encourages us – and especially women – to define ourselves by our bodies. How sexy they are, how well they fit into society's narrow mould of what is 'attractive', and how capable they are of carrying out our womanly role (bearing children). It's no wonder, then, that so many of us have difficult relationships with our bodies, when they stubbornly fall short of our expectations. It's no wonder that so many of us have sat in front of the mirror, looked at our reflections, and cried.

I hadn't delivered my daughter vaginally, and it was only a few years later, after reading Oprah Winfrey's book, *What I Know For Sure,* that I understood where this feeling had come from: I believed my body had let me down. Rather than praising myself for the amazing feat of creating new life, my body became a symbol of failure and I channelled my self-loathing into it. Wasn't giving birth what we were made for? Why had my body let me down when I needed it most? Seeing this new body that I didn't recognise, I came to the dawning realisation that I had given up on my whole life; my attractiveness (and all the pleasures that came with that), my sense of self, my sense of worth. I knew instinctively that I loved my child (I had wanted a baby from a very young age), but it was like something had been traded off. I loved my daughter, and I hated myself.

No one knew about my self-loathing at that time, because I didn't tell anyone. I thought that admitting my flaws and failures would make me seem self-absorbed, or like a bad mother. I didn't want to give the hatred I had for myself any airtime, thinking that if I don't speak about it, it might go away, on its own. My husband, friends and family only saw what I wanted them to see – that I was giddily embracing new motherhood; confident and glowing. But behind closed doors, I was chastising my body, angry at my soft, deflated stomach and big thighs for betraying me. After that occasion, I avoided mirrors as much as I could. I wouldn't walk around naked in front of my husband; something I'd always done without thinking suddenly became fraught with shame. It's normal to feel unsure about sex in the early stages of new motherhood, but my body-hatred took that to another level, and the thought of restarting erotic intimacy terrified me.

Looking back on myself then, I feel unbelievably sad. I wish I could hug 29-year-old Nat and tell her that the social acceptability of her body and her self-worth are not the same thing. But I don't blame her for having those feelings, or for the lack of feelings. I mean, I still feel like that sometimes too, but now I'm able to pull myself out of it. All of those emotions that came flooding while I sat there on the bed were just the accumulation of three decades' worth of social conditioning. Of being taught that women's bodies are more important than our brains, our personalities, our resilience ... pretty much everything about us. Of believing that the purpose of our bodies is to be sexually attractive to the opposite sex (which, I believed, mine no longer was) and to give birth (which I felt like I hadn't even managed).

Ultimately, we live in a culture that encourages women to hate themselves, and seeing my new post-baby body meant those feelings collapsed on top of me like an avalanche.

*

Sometimes, I yearn for my childhood innocence; it was one of the only periods in my life where I wasn't consciously aware of my body on a daily basis. It was just the skin I lived in, and I grew up with very few feelings about my weight, or size. My mum never restricted what food I could eat, or commented on my body, or told me I needed to exercise, so I often think I grew up in some kind of body-hatred-free utopia. But when I dig a little deeper into my memories, I can see that Mum was very focused on her own body. She didn't inflict this on me, at least not intentionally, but her feelings were ever-present. She always seemed to be on some kind of strict diet. There was one called the cabbage soup diet, and I can still remember the disgusting smell wafting through the house. I don't remember her ever being particularly overweight when I was a kid, but she was prescribed diet pills from the doctor and her weight did fluctuate from the yo-yo dieting and pills. I have now learned that, in the 1980s, it was pretty standard for women to be prescribed appetite-suppressing amphetamine-like drugs.

Without even realising it, I was absorbing ideas about the value of womanhood from a young age. Research has shown that women pass on their body issues to their children, and I am sure this happened to me. Alongside caring about her make-up and hair, my mum, like most women, was preoccupied with the appearance of her body. I learned that, as a woman, keeping yourself beautiful was expected and necessary – and a huge part of that involved keeping your body trim. She restricted herself so that she would be smaller, because women should move through the world taking up as little space as possible, while being delectable to the male gaze.

As a child, I loved old Hollywood movies. After watching *Some Like It Hot*, I became completely obsessed with Marilyn Monroe. I'm not sure if I wanted to fuck her, be her, or be her best friend – I suspect it was probably all three. To me, she was the epitome of sexiness. She had blonde hair (essential), big boobs (vital) and an hourglass figure with the tiniest waist. I loved the fact she was damaged but still so very beautiful; I read books about her, and had posters of her plastered on my wall. She was everything I wanted to be.

Of course, Marilyn was an icon – I idolised her and knew I could never measure up to how beautiful she was. Nor would I ever look like actresses Julia Roberts or Meg Ryan, or supermodels like Cindy Crawford and Elle Macpherson. They were goddess-like, perfect women. Yet, the messages I received from all corners of popular and consumer culture insisted that I should at least try. The adverts that saturated my favourite TV shows were full of razors and moisturisers, suggesting that the perfect female body should be silky smooth and wrinkle-free. The magazines I pored over told me how to diet, exercise and essentially punish myself (as my mother had always done) – all for the purpose of snaring and keeping a man. Before I hit puberty, these ideas had seeped into my blood. I believed it was a woman's duty to have as close to a perfect body as possible.

I dreamed of growing up to have a tiny waist and big boobs. I wanted slim, silky legs, and toned, slender arms. I wanted juicy, kissable lips, and I wished I had a petite, delicate nose, lovely almond-shaped eyes and long silky hair that would swish around when I walked. Many of these qualities were ones I knew I would never possess. I hated my features that accentuated the fact I'm not white; I thought my nose was too wide and too flat, and I viewed my hair to be frizzy and unruly (this was how the hair-care adverts described it, after all). As I entered my teens and became more conscious of my body, I thought my back arched too much, drawing attention to my bigger bum (which, at the time, was *not* a good thing). I had very few Black role models – there was Naomi Campbell, but she always seemed to be characterised as the 'difficult one' and wasn't someone I believed I should look up to. I struggled growing up mixed-race. I had a lot of identity issues; I wished I was white and blonde, more than anything else. I knew there was nothing I could do about it, but this overriding sense that my body and how I looked wasn't good enough hugely impacted my self-esteem.

But there was a contradiction at play, too. I noticed how Black bodies – and especially mixed-race, light-skinned bodies – were fetishised. I can vividly remember watching one of Harry Enfield's 'The Slobs' sketches, where Kathy Burke's character talked about how she wanted a 'brown baby'. This idea was repeated on one of my favourite shows,

Absolutely Fabulous, when Saffy gave birth to a mixed-race baby girl, and her mother Eddie (played by Jennifer Saunders) declared her granddaughter a fabulous fashion accessory, calling her 'the Chanel of babies'. I'd hear white women make this comment – genuinely – in real life, for years. It always seemed odd to me that my mixed-race features were simultaneously considered ugly by mainstream culture, and also given some kind of weird mythical glorification. I'm sure it's something to do with the way our society values 'exotic' looks, but only as a source of entertainment or intrigue.

I also noticed the continued fetishisation of Black men. I can remember girls at my school giggling about Black men having bigger dicks, and, as I grew up, this idea popped up all the time in porn too. Although it might seem like a positive stereotype on the surface, I'm sure this idea is rooted in the slave era; in the idea that Black men are sexually aggressive or out of control. And despite being culturally deemed less attractive than white women, I know that Black women's bodies have been sexualised as a hangover from the slave era too, when their bodies were – quite literally – owned, and used, by white men (and their wives). The messaging has always suggested that Black women can be the object of lust, but not love. Internalising all of these conflicting ideas was confronting and confusing.

It's strange, really, how you forget compliments almost as soon as someone makes one, but a negative remark can stick with you for a lifetime. When I was a teenager, my mum's friend told me I had a great figure – 'except for your thighs'. A boy at school called me a Black bitch. Another kid told me my mouth was too big and wide, whenever I smiled or laughed. These insults, these direct assaults on my body and race, have stayed with me ever since. For each one, I'd add to the list of things I wished I could change about myself: flatter tummy, bigger boobs, smaller thighs, more 'delicate' facial features. I understood that striving towards a perfect body was essential for social acceptance. The boys at school would maliciously tease the girls they deemed to be 'fat' or flat-chested; they'd make jokes at their expense, suggesting that no one would ever want to have sex with them. It was awful. But I know that these were society's ideas that had seeped into their blood, too. It was widely believed that body fat was undesirable, and rendered you unfuckable.

I'd hear women gossiping about other women who had 'let themselves go'; women who had put on weight and had stopped actively caring about their appearance. These insults became deeply ingrained in my consciousness and made me incredibly judgemental. Even when I entered adulthood, I'd see women, and I would sneer and think, 'how can her husband still want to fuck her? Why didn't she keep herself in better shape for her man?' I feel physically sick admitting that, because it's so cruel and so wrong. But I am a product of patriarchal society – I have absorbed these misogynistic ideas just as much as anyone else. I had always been shown that women were there to look pretty, to serve men sexually and socially. So when other women fell short of that requirement, it felt like a betrayal. Although, I guess it was also one less woman for me to compete against.

Bodies

Moving through my teens, worries about my body weight and shape were already enough to contend with. But as I started to watch more porn and have sex, I became self-conscious about my genitals and my body hair. My vulva seemed to look different to the ones I had seen in biology textbooks and in porn; the lips seemed darker, and the inside was a different shade still. I'd fret about the smell too, which led me to use odour-controlling products that would give me thrush. I constantly worried about whether I was abnormal. Clearly, I'm not the only one who has felt, or feels, this way. In 2019, lifestyle news website Refinery29 carried out a survey with 3,670 respondents, finding that 48% of women had concerns about the appearance of their vulva; they were worried about the size (64%), shape (60%) and colour (30%). Perhaps most upsettingly, 32% of the women said they had been made to feel like their vagina was not 'normal'. When the women were asked to cite where this came from, porn came up repeatedly. It's understandable that seeing very similar, tucked-away, pink vaginas in porn would make women feel that there's something wrong with them down there.

Plus, the vulvas in porn were almost always hairless. And this, no doubt, has led men to believe that untamed female pubic hair is dirty and disgusting. My first boyfriend would never make me feel bad about how my genitals looked – except when I hadn't recently shaved. He would almost recoil in horror. Even at the time, I found it completely bizarre. I think, from growing up and seeing my mum's bush, I understood that not having any hair at all is almost like looking like a child. I remember being pretty excited when my pubes started to sprout, because I felt like I'd finally become a grown-up. Even though the gorgeous women in porn removed all their hair, something felt icky about it. So instead, I would get a wax but leave a strip, a tiny bit of hair just above the vulva. I bowed down to the expectation of removing body hair, but I suppose that was my little strip of rebellion.

Despite all the fear and expectation surrounding having the 'perfect' toned, trim, neat, hairless body, I also knew that my physicality was sexual currency. And I planned to use it. Throughout my teens and twenties, I was extremely preoccupied with how I looked. Feeling attractive to the opposite sex – whether it was my boyfriend at the time, or random men who crossed my path – was overwhelmingly important to me. I studied Psychology at university and trained to be a midwife after I came back from travelling. I wanted to be intellectual and financially self-sufficient and feel like I was doing something purposeful in life. But I think I always believed, deep down, that I would never be much more than my appearance. My true value would always be in how I looked.

As I had first discovered in the supermarket aged 11, my body was a source of power. Despite my ever-present hang-ups, I knew I could make my body look desirable. For nights out, I'd squeeze into the most revealing clothes to accentuate my boobs and show off my figure. My favourite outfit was a tight brown Lycra dress, with a massive slit up the side and big gaping holes down the middle. I thought I looked amazing in it and I loved the attention it brought. One of the first times I went clubbing with a friend, using borrowed fake IDs aged 16, we wore tiny little white lace dresses with our thongs visible underneath. I can still remember the looks we received from the men in the club; they were wide-eyed and ravenous. I had a boyfriend at the time so I wasn't even trying to hook up – but the attention itself was enough of a buzz.

I loved the idea of turning heads; it was like a hit of dopamine and validation that made me feel valuable and wanted. I liked being wolf-whistled. I liked being looked at. As a feminist now, I find it difficult to admit that. In theory, I feel angry that men feel entitled to approach and interrupt women to comment on their bodies or make them feel like they're sexual objects. What gives them the right to infringe on a woman's personal space to comment on her appearance? But, in reality, it didn't always feel so negative. Seeing as we've been taught to believe that attractiveness is the most important thing in life, it's unsurprising that this kind of unwanted attention can still make us feel good. It's almost like a reminder that we're doing it right. Of course, it could be intimidating sometimes; I was definitely more afraid than flattered if a man approached me late at night. But feeling sexy and attractive was very important to me.

I made it through my teens without exercising much, and eating whatever I wanted. Despite my insecurities, I knew my svelte figure could attract that attention I craved. But I first noticed my body changing when I was travelling around South East Asia and Australia in my early twenties. I was having so much fun – eating packet noodles or chips all day and drinking all night. But one day, I looked at pictures of myself on the beach that my friend had taken and realised I looked bigger than I ever had. I suddenly became conscious of the fact my body was growing and changing, and it made me feel sick. I took up running straight away, doing laps of Bondi Beach in the burning sun. I absolutely hated running so I probably only did it once or twice at the most – but still, something inside me shifted. I became self-conscious about what I wore, and tried to scale back on the carbs I had been eating. I felt ashamed of myself.

That socially approved female self-hatred – drilled into me from years of adverts, movies and flippant remarks – began to firmly take hold. My self-consciousness about my body impacted the sex I was having. By that point, I had been with my college boyfriend for a few years, and I was completely comfortable around him. Except, during sex, I was afraid that he'd be disgusted by me. I'd fixate on whether a sex position would accentuate my stomach rolls, and I'd worry about whether my cellulite was visible. One of my favourite sex positions involved lying on my back with my legs up; I liked the deepness and the way it felt inside. But this is a terrible position if you're worried about your body. We'd start having sex and my legs would creep up, and the sensation would get better and better, but then I'd see the fat bunch in small mounds across my torso, and it would be enough to stop me enjoying what was happening. I couldn't get my own appearance out of my head, and it prevented me from being present. I wish I could have stayed in the moment and enjoyed the pleasurable experience, but I couldn't. I was fucked (literally) by how society had made me feel.

Bodies

And it's not that my partner ever made me feel bad about how I looked – in fact, it was quite the opposite. I know he didn't give a shit about my cellulite or stretch marks, and he'd constantly tell me that I had great tits and that he liked my butt. But the praise never really landed. In my head, I'd be wishing my tits were perkier, and my bum was rounder. I think you can be given all the compliments in the world, but if you're not feeling good about your body, they just won't sink in. There was a complete disconnect between what he thought about me, and how I viewed myself. I wish I could've seen myself from his point of view, as someone who loved me, instead of always viewing myself through the lens of what I thought I 'should' be.

Although I always worried about my weight, I generally didn't bow down too much to diet culture. I always felt that balance was the best approach, and tried not to give in to diet fads. Until, of course, my wedding. For some reason, we're taught that our wedding day should be the peak of our physical attractiveness. I'm sure it has something to do with society's obsession with brides more broadly – it's like the last time women are angelic and pure, before we're handed over to a man to fulfil our duty (as a good house-wife and a baby-making machine). Whatever the reason, I was intent on being skinny for my big day. As soon as we set the date, I signed up to the gym for the first time and hired a personal trainer who put me on a diet plan – which basic-ally consisted of eating pork belly for breakfast, lunch and dinner. At the same time, she'd have me doing intermittent training and weights. I started shedding the pounds. But honestly, I was miserable. I was grumpy all the time – and now I realise I was hangry (hungry and angry – the lethal combination). But, I had to be my 'ideal' figure and weight in time for my wedding. When I look back on the pictures from that day, I marvel at how skinny I was, but I don't think I looked my best. And I know I didn't feel it either. Yes, I was happy and in love, but deep down, I felt tired and starved. That was the last time I ever followed a strict diet regime.

Becoming pregnant for the first time was a totally different story. It was the first time since childhood that I felt free to live inside my body, rather than constantly worrying about how I looked. As my belly swelled into a big balloon, I knew it was just doing its job: creating new life. For the first time ever I didn't suck in my stomach, because I physically couldn't, and it felt great. I know that some people suffer from more extreme body issues during pregnancy, but for me, it was a wonderful time. I was proud of how my body was growing. But those feelings of freedom came crashing down once I gave birth, and stared at my naked body that day in the mirror. The brief respite from body hang-ups during pregnancy was simply the calm before the storm. Post-baby, my body became my number one enemy. I hid it as much as I could behind baggier clothes. I felt completely disconnected from it – like it wasn't mine. As a result, sex felt disconnected too. When my husband and I started having sex again, I insisted on doing it with the lights off. I didn't want to look at my own body, let alone have him look at it. I was completely consumed with hatred for how I looked.

In her incredible memoir, *Untamed*, writer Glennon Doyle described how her body issues came from 'breathing misogynistic air'.

'Self-hatred is harder to unlearn than it is to learn,' she wrote. 'It is difficult for a woman to be healthy in a culture that is still so very sick.'

So much clicked into place when I read those lines. I – and so many other women – have been poisoned by the culture we live in; a culture that continues to place far too much emphasis on how our bodies look. Social media and billboards are saturated with adverts for diet products claiming to make you skinnier. Porn is still overwhelmingly full of slim, hairless women with big breasts. And I can't see there being a huge change any time soon, because hating our bodies – and constantly striving towards impossible standards – is big business. Consumerism is pretty much founded on it. Why would we buy slimming underwear, or hair removal cream, or gym memberships, if we felt happy and content with ourselves?

In *The Beauty Myth*, an iconic feminist manifesto published in 1990, author Naomi Wolf argued that patriarchal society and consumer culture has led women to believe that our value lies in how we look. Forcing women to become preoccupied with the appearance of their bodies, she suggested, was holding women back from achieving their true potential, and being accepted in society. More than 30 years on from the publication of *The Beauty Myth*, there's even more money to be made off the backs of self-hating women, and it feels more relevant than ever.

And it's not just women who have to confront unrealistic images about bodies – I know there's so much pressure for men to 'bulk'; to appear big, strong and muscular. The messaging is: women should take up less space, and men should take up more. These ideas about what 'good' bodies look like are making everyone sick. They're making us judgemental and insecure. And they're completely fucking up our sexual pleasure.

It's only really in the last 100 years that showing skin in public has been socially acceptable. Shorter, sleeveless dresses came into fashion in the 1920s, and miniskirts didn't become popularised until the 1960s. We have attached so much social and sexual emphasis to women's bodies, so, unsurprisingly, it's a huge act of vulnerability to show our unbridled, naked selves to someone else. This is the first hurdle in sexual intimacy – so if we can't even allow ourselves to be vulnerable in our nakedness, to say 'this is who I am' from a place of acceptance and love, then how can we ever be vulnerable enough to surrender to sexual pleasure? It's unsurprising that I found sex so challenging when I was struggling with my body image. My shame prevented me from experiencing vulnerability, and vulnerability prevented me from experiencing enjoyment. How can our bodies feel what we want them to feel if we're not even comfortable inside our own skin? It was only once I learned to accept and embrace my body that I started having my best sex ever.

*

The digital world gets a really bad rap when it comes to body confidence. After all, social media is full of celebrities and influencers with 'perfect' bodies, and it's often hard to distinguish between what is real and what is heavily edited.

Bodies

It's bad enough that we compare ourselves to people who can afford (and have time for) the most expensive trainers, nutritionists and surgery. But when it's obvious that famous women – even the most Amazonian and gorgeous models – edit their pictures to make their waists seem even smaller and their legs even longer, it really can feel like a losing game. I truly believe that every time you digitally alter yourself, you are losing a piece of who you really are. You're damaging your soul. And, in turn, those false images damage the self-esteem of everyone who sees them. They give thousands of women impossible standards to compare themselves against. I think images like this need to have warning signs, or they should be banned altogether. It's corrosive and extremely problematic.

But although social media can be the very worst place to go for body confidence, it can also be the best – as long as you curate your feed correctly. In fact, my own journey towards loving my body began by discovering the body positivity movement on Instagram. This community sprang up partly in response to these heavily edited online images, as a way of saying that all women are worthy of having a positive body image, no matter what the societally accepted ideas of beauty are. This resonated with me because I felt that my post-motherhood body would simply never match up to the models and influencers I was seeing everywhere. It's wild that these kinds of images are even presented as the norm, considering the average clothes size of women in the UK is a 16. I realised I was looking in all the wrong places to feel valid and accepted. So I started following people like Megan Jayne Crabbe (@meganjaynecrabbe, formerly known as bodyposipanda), Stephanie Yeboah (@stephanieyeboah) and Grace Victory (@gracefvictory); I sought out women who proudly posted pictures of their bodies, stretch marks, cellulite and facial and body hair. It was the first time my world had opened up to the mere suggestion that I could be okay, comfortable or even happy with my body. I thought: if these incredible women, of all different shapes and sizes, can expose themselves like that and still feel confident, then why can't I?

Although sharing pictures of my body online feels like second nature now, I can still remember the first time I showed myself in a revealing and realistic way online. It was seven or eight years ago, and it felt like a huge, momentous occasion. Despite finding the body positivity community online, it definitely wasn't as big as it is now – and I worried about how people would react. I feared insults and back-lash. It was a picture of me wearing a revealing denim pinafore dress with no underwear and a lot of boob on display. Before I clicked 'post', I felt physically sick. But the response was absolutely amazing. People told me that my post had made them feel better about their own bodies; that it was so refreshing to see women taking ownership of their body types, and feeling proud to have them. When I looked at that picture, I didn't feel ashamed of how I looked. I actually felt proud. Proud that I had helped so many people feel seen and represented. Proud that this body was mine.

It was a game-changer and completely shaped the content I put out to this day. I felt encouraged and supported to carry on being vulnerable. I wanted to keep on showing my body in all its wonderful reality, without sucking in my stomach, or posing only at the most stereotypically 'flattering' angles. I refused to wear clothes that I've always been told are best to compliment my shape (i.e. baggy and dark), and have always tried to encourage my followers to wear what the fuck they like. You don't need to have a particular body shape to wear shorts or a crop top. Everyone has a right to enjoy their own body, and dress it however they please.

Now, I post revealing and honest photos of my body regularly. I think it's so important that when people flick through Instagram, among all the airbrushed perfection, they also see images of bodies that look like theirs: full of texture and life. In 2020, I posted an image of me excitedly holding a mirror up to my vulva, and it lost me a ton of followers. I understood. This image would've probably made me shocked, or annoyed, a few years ago. I would've thought: why can't they keep some things private? Why do they have to be such an exhibitionist? But I was so proud to show this image because I had spent such a long time being ashamed of my own vulva. But, finally, I realised that our bodies are there to be celebrated. There's absolutely no shame in a woman being ecstatic while looking at her own body parts in the mirror. Thankfully, the positive response was much greater than the backlash. And, in 2021, I posed for a completely naked photo shoot with the stunning photographer Alexandra Cameron (@alex_cameron), where I squeezed my tummy and didn't even try to hide my body hair, or distort my body into positions to look skinnier. Looking at those images now makes me emotional, because I know just how much self-hatred I had to overcome to get there.

I also decided that I would never digitally edit or distort my body in photos, even if it feels excruciatingly painful to post an image that isn't 'perfect'. Even though it might look easy for me to share these parts of myself, I'm still – in the words of Glennon – breathing in those misogynistic toxins. Just like anyone else, my body confidence fluctuates; sometimes I feel like a goddess, and other times, my self-esteem is on the floor and I feel disgusting. But I am learning to make space for both of those feelings. It's just not realistic to expect to love our bodies 100% of the time. Asking that of ourselves can actually increase pressure, and make us feel worse.

Though, I know there's a correlation between the times when I feel confident about my body, and the quality of sex I have. When I perceive myself as beautiful, strong and sexy, it allows me to open myself up to intimacy and sexual pleasure. It doesn't matter how much my partner tells me that they like the way I look, I won't ever really feel it unless those compliments are coming from within. Whenever my internal dialogue is being nasty and judgemental – like rudely commenting on the size of my thighs or stomach, or telling me I'm disgusting and no one will ever love me – I try to remind myself that this voice is a remnant of the misogynistic and oppressive world I've grown up in. It does not determine my worth. Whenever those thoughts begin to surface, I think: 'would you speak to your child self like this?' I picture myself as a kid, while I hurl those insults at myself. I imagine the tears in her eyes; the sadness she must be feeling. I would never want my own kids to feel that way, so I know I need to extend the same kindness to myself.

Bodies

The way we view 'ideal' bodies is fucking arbitrary anyway. Throughout history, different body features have been viewed as more attractive at different times; you only have to look at Renaissance paintings to see that curvy, pear-shaped figures were perceived as the most beautiful. Yet, in the 1990s, we saw the emergence of 'heroin chic', where stick-thinness was viewed as the epitome of beauty. The features that distinguished my blackness – like my bigger bum and lips – were considered unattractive when I was young but are now seen as the most sexually attractive and desirable assets you can have. Sure, the fetishisation of these features is still problematic, but it just shows that beauty ideals change all the time, so it's an impossible task to keep on chasing them. It's transient and superficial. You may as well just enjoy living in the body you're in right now.

I know many people prefer the term 'body neutrality' to 'body positivity'; it's the idea that we should focus on what our bodies can do, rather than what they look like. Essentially, the purpose is to remove the obsession with the aesthetics of our bodies so that we can find freedom. I think it's a noble idea, and I definitely try to apply elements of this thinking to my own life – whenever I feel bad about my stomach or thighs, I remember that this is the body that housed both my daughters, and that's a real fucking miracle. However, I don't think it's realistic to have this mentality all of the time. We move through the world preoccupied by the appearance of things – whether that's a new wallpaper colour, or the attractiveness of a potential partner. I don't think we can really deny that aesthetics matter to us. I think it's about acknowledging that, but not allowing it to take over.

If you're trying to reach a place of body acceptance, I recommend throwing away your weighing scales. You are so much more than a number – body confidence should always come from how you feel, not how much you weigh. I used to let the numbers dictate my day. If I had lost a couple of pounds, I knew I'd have a good day. Avoiding diet culture and fostering a balanced approach to food and exercise helps too. I eat what I feel my body needs (whether that's a fresh salad or a massive burger) – restricting foods has only ever made me crave them more. Exercise for me is just movement that feels good and gets my endorphins rushing – most of the time, it's dancing. I fucking love going to dance classes – it's the only exercise I do that I don't clock watch. The time just goes, I'm not praying for it to end; in fact, the complete opposite, and I'm drenched with sweat. But I avoid making adjustments to my food intake or exercise in order to lose weight. Mostly because I know my weight will fluctuate no matter what I'm doing. I'm much more secure, now, in the knowledge that fluctuation is natural and normal.

That's not to say I don't still get down if I gain weight. I do. Noticing that my weight has increased can often send me into a spiral of self-hatred and shame. I think we need to allow ourselves to feel those feelings too. Noticing any change in your body – whether that's gaining weight, losing it, getting bigger boobs or seeing stretch marks appear – can feel like the loss of a person you once were. It's okay to mourn that version of yourself. You're so intimately connected with your own body, so it's natural to miss what you used to look like. Forgive yourself for that. But you can also look in the mirror at your new body and say, 'nice to meet you. I know I will grow to love you, too. Just give me a minute.'

It's unsurprising that my post-baby body felt like a loss; it was indicative of me growing older. In our society, we place so much value on youth and thinness that getting older can feel like we're failing as women. We've been taught that it's not okay or normal to grow old, hence the growing movement for having Botox and plastic surgery to try to look young for as long as possible. I do struggle with the idea of getting older. Every time I see a new wrinkle on my face, I squirm a little. I even tried Botox once, even though it goes against my core values, because I do sometimes buckle under the pressure of society's standards. I'm happy with how I am at the moment, but I wouldn't rule out getting it again. Though, I try to remember that with age comes experience and wisdom. My body holds 40 years of fun, happiness, sadness, anxiety, excitement and lessons learned. That's pretty fucking valuable. Growing old is a bloody honour that not everyone gets.

Today, right now, I feel a deep love for my body. I don't like it all the time, but that's just like any important relationship in your life. There will be ups and downs, and part of love means accepting the good and the bad. I still wax and shave; I like my skin to look soft and smooth. I know it's impossible to fully disconnect from the messaging we've been fed throughout the years. I can only hope that my girls grow up with fewer of these fires to fight. I make a conscious effort to never talk about my body in front of my daughters, especially not in a denigrating way.

Even if the world continues to tell them that they're not good enough (which I'm sure it will), I hope that seeing their mother love and embrace her body will help in some small way.

My body is fucking incredible really – it has given me purpose, pleasure and children; it is beautiful and delicious, and when society (or that niggling voice inside my head) tries to tell me otherwise, I tell it firmly to fuck off. And body confidence really is the key to great sex. If we want to enjoy all the pleasure that comes with other people's bodies, we need to learn to enjoy our own. We have to find a home inside ourselves, otherwise we'll feel completely disconnected from the sensations that can swirl within. Body confidence is a journey I'm still very much on, but I'm no longer fighting my body. I know that we're on the same team. So when you next look in the mirror, even if you hate what you see, I want you to flip the script. I want you to remember that your body is your home. I want you to look at that beautiful, unique and wondrous body – the skin and bones that belong to you, and you alone – and smile.

What I've learned about body acceptance and confidence:

- We will live in our bodies for our whole lives – we must learn to treat them with kindness and respect. Try repeating this affirmation to yourself in front of the mirror each morning: 'Today I accept my body for what it is, and what it isn't. For what it can do, and what it can't do.' There is freedom in the realisation that, today, your body is what it is, and there's nothing you can do to change that. You might as well use your time and energy thinking about other things.

- I've gone through life saying things like, 'when I've lost a stone, I will get that tattoo/buy that dress/wear a bikini.' Don't wait for your body to change in order to be happy. Do that thing now.

- During sex, how our bodies look should be the least of our worries. Feeling and connecting are much more important to focus on. I avoid focusing on my body by imagining sexy scenarios in my head, or closing my eyes and mindfully tuning into the sensation running through my body.

- Follow people online who support you to feel good in the skin you're in. My favourites are Scotty Thee Sexfluencer (@scottyunfamous) and Trina Nicole (@itstrinanicole). If you need to mute or unfollow people (even if they're your friends) because they post body-related content that triggers you, do it.

- Create clear boundaries with people who make you feel bad about your body. If your parents, partner or friends make disparaging remarks about your body, tell them: 'I am trying to heal and love myself. Please do not insult my body like that.' If they still do, it could be worth thinking about whether there's room for that person in your life. You deserve to be loved and treasured, whatever your size or shape.

- In our society, I believe women have been taught about our bodies as a control tactic to stop us thinking about things like work, politics, and other matters of importance. Rail against this by caring and thinking deeply about other things. Find your purpose. Embrace your sexuality. These tiny acts of rebellion add up to revolution.

6

Masturbation

The first time I started masturbating, consciously and intentionally, I was in my early thirties. I was in the midst of a period of deep self-loathing – I thought my altered, post-baby body was devastatingly ugly, which was badly affecting my sex life with my husband. I was struggling with my sense of self and didn't know how to connect. But at the same time, becoming a mother gave me a deep urge to learn more about – and try to accept – myself, so I started seeking out anything that could boost my self-esteem. I was becoming more engaged with body positivity and sex positivity online, and I learned that touching myself could actually be an act of self-love. So, being in desperate need of self-love, I decided to try.

In the middle of the day, when my husband was at work and my baby was asleep, I'd lie on my bed and start touching myself. At first, I felt self-conscious; I would look around expecting someone to poke their head around the corner. I'd check for hidden cameras pointing at me, nestled within the books on the shelf, filming videos that would prove, once and for all, that I was dirty and disgusting. And even after dismissing those irrational thoughts, I still found it difficult. I'd find a movement that felt good, and then intrusive thoughts would rush into my brain, telling me to pick up a prescription or remember to buy bin bags. I found it hard to switch off and focus on the feelings. Often, I'd become annoyed and give up, having worked up a bit of a sweat. Yet I persevered, because those moments of sensation seemed to be worth trying for.

Eventually, after a lot of trial and error, I started to give myself orgasms. They started off little at first. They would often creep up slowly, and then poof, they'd fizzle out quickly like a candle had just been blown out, slightly disappointingly but better than nothing. As I started to relax more, the orgasms got better and better, and then one day, out of nowhere, I had the kind of full-body, scream-out-loud, body-shuddering orgasm I didn't even know was possible (but always hoped was). I was wide-eyed with amazement, and it felt revolutionary. It was as if I'd discovered a magic potion I could drink whenever I wanted to feel euphoric. I realised that I didn't have to rely on anyone, that I could make myself feel good alone. Before that point, I'd only known sexual pleasure when other people handed it to me; when they'd given me permission. This was the first time I was completely autonomous in my own desire. I could make myself come! It felt sexy and delicious and powerful. It was a beautiful realisation; one that should've happened many years before.

Masturbation

I know, I know: I'm a very late bloomer. According to a Swedish study, the average age girls start masturbating is 13 years old, no doubt in line with the sexual urges of puberty. But the same study also found that 15% of women had never masturbated at all (compared to just 1% of men) so, up until a decade ago, I would've been in that category. I can't be the only woman who felt that masturbation wasn't 'for' me. Because the very concept of female masturbation was – and still is – almost synonymous with the idea of shame. I believed it was dirty and immoral; definitely not something that 'good girls' would do.

But I only learned these social cues when, as a teenager, I found out what masturbation actually was. Before that, I think I always knew, deep down, that rubbing things against my vulva felt good. When I was around six or seven, I had a particular affinity for humping teddies. I used to do it at my friend's house, when our mums were busy chatting downstairs. My friend's bed was covered with a shitload of teddies. I'm not sure how or why it started – I imagine we made up some kind of make-believe game to justify it – but we'd pick a teddy each and hump it, or rub it against ourselves. Sometimes, we'd even rub against each other, if we were feeling particularly risqué. We clearly didn't have enough sexual awareness to attach any kind of erotic significance to what we were doing, but somehow we knew it was something our mums shouldn't know about, that it should be done in secret. If we heard them call our names, saying it was time to leave, we'd immediately push the teddies away, rearrange our dishevelled clothing and run out of the room, flush-faced.

As a teenager, I learned why these actions were so shameful. In school, masturbating – or, wanking – was widely talked about among the boys. I always believed it was something they physically had to do – to release tension or to lighten up their heavy balls, or something – and it was just part of being male. Boys would show off about how much they wanked, beaming with pride about the strength of their right arms. But for girls, it was a completely different story. Someone told me that masturbating could make girls go blind. I've recently learned this is a myth that has existed since the early nineteenth century, alongside others, like it causing infertility, mental health issues and sexual dysfunction. I also learned that women in the Victorian period were regularly sent off to asylums if they were found to touch themselves, because deviant female sexuality was believed to be a sign of 'hysteria'. What a fucking joke that is.

Clearly, these old legends hadn't quite disappeared. Although I didn't believe I'd go blind in a literal sense, I did think that touching myself could have disastrous consequences. I thought that, if anyone found out I'd done it, I'd be maligned, almost like being a paedophile. After all, rumours circulated about girls who wanked; in the same way sluts were outcasted for being 'too' sexual, any girl who wanked was believed to be disgusting, unable to keep her urges in check. I didn't want to be that kind of girl.

It's hard to pinpoint where and why female masturbation became so entwined with morality, but the taboo dates back thousands of years. Of course, many religions including Christianity condemn all forms of masturbation (even for men), believing that sexual pleasure is a sin and should be reserved for the sanctity of having babies within marriage. But, clearly, the majority of men in today's society don't have the same level of shame attached to masturbation. A 2018 study by TENGA found that 96% of men said that they masturbate, compared to 78% of women. I'm sure that this figure is so much lower because the stigma is still so high for women, and it comes back to all the fucked-up notions we have about female purity. Desiring, wanting, and chasing pleasure has long been perceived as dirty, and even evil. By contrast, these qualities in men are simply signs of good old red-blooded masculinity. Throughout history, there have always been huge double standards about the way men are praised and women are vilified for having the exact same wants and urges. We might have moved on in a lot of ways – in Western culture, women are no longer defamed for shagging before marriage – but our attitudes to masturbation are like a lingering hangover from those times. Female masturbation is tied up with goodness in a way that it simply isn't for men. So it's no wonder, really, that I emerged into adulthood afraid of touching my own genitals.

As I started having sex, those pleasurable feelings from humping teddies were long-forgotten. Pleasure became something completely different – it wasn't about me any more. When I was a kid, I was free – led by my own innate needs. Now, I had the weight of expectation on me. Other people's desires and needs became more important, and it was my socialised role as a woman to fulfil them. This applied to my life more generally, but especially during sex. It's hard to pinpoint the exact moment I started to forget about myself. When did I stop allowing myself to explore nice feelings, to be led by my own intrinsic wants? When did I stop listening to myself? In a strange way, my own voice got smaller and smaller as I grew.

I'm sure some of my friends at school did masturbate, but I definitely didn't know about it. To be honest, if a friend had told me at the time that she wanked, I'd probably be disgusted – so I'm not surprised I was never told. We would turn our noses up at the very idea of touching ourselves, yet we'd chase after any finger-action if it came from a boy. It's weird, really, that having other people's dirty fingers go near our vulvas was somehow safer, less sullying, than using our own. But that's just the way it was.

Alongside being the domain of dirty, evil girls, self-pleasure was also for the lonely. After all, why would you need to give yourself sexual kicks when you could get them from your boyfriend? As someone who always craved the security of a relationship, I felt I would never *need* to do that to myself. It was embarrassing to seek satisfaction solo. Even when I started learning more about feminism and sexuality in my twenties, and I started to understand that maybe masturbating isn't quite as disgraceful as I'd been led to believe, I still didn't think I needed to do it. I had a long-term partner, he had a penis – what else could I possibly want from my sex life? It baffles me, now, to think about how much time I spent in showers, baths, in bed, completely oblivious to the magical clitoris attached to my body, not realising what I could feel if I dared to touch it.

*

Masturbation

It was only when partnered sex was off the table (temporarily – because my body confidence was just too low to get intimate with my husband) that I decided to give masturbation a go. I had spent a long time unpacking all my shame around it. I'd scroll through reassuring Instagram posts that told me, again and again, that masturbation was actually a natural, and even a beneficial, part of being a woman. These posts forced me to question all the stories I had told myself. Why *did* I think masturbation was so bad? What did I actually think might happen to me if I tried it? I realised that I didn't actually have answers to any of these questions; not legitimate ones, anyway. If you think something is bad, but you can't explain why it's bad in a way that aligns with your overall values and lifestyle, then, in all likelihood, it's probably just social conditioning you've been fed. I quickly realised that everything I had previously believed was essentially built on outdated religious ideals, fucked-up notions of purity and the demonisation of female sexuality. Once I let go of all that shit, I thought: 'what's stopping me?'

Yet, putting my fingers near my vulva for the first few times made me feel guilty. I think I felt, ever so slightly, that I was betraying my husband – like I was cheating on him, or that I had misled him with my whole 'good girl' act. I felt like I was betraying my upbringing, too; I imagined the images of Jesus on stained-glass windows in my Catholic school looking down on me. Numerous uncomfortable feelings swarmed inside me, and I had to squeeze my eyes shut and try to block all of it out. It was hard. But, reaching the other side, it was worth it.

Frankly, once I got started, and realised just how awesome wanking actually was, I simply couldn't stop. I would do it at every opportunity; whenever I had some private time. I just thought: how have I been missing this? How did I not realise that all this potential for joy was at my literal fingertips?

After a few months, I decided to branch out from my own hands. I started to invest in some sex toys. I was pretty nervous about levelling up my masturbation game, especially because I had some negative pre-conceived ideas about what sex toys were. I remembered finding a dildo in my mum's underwear drawer when I was a child. It was a big black plastic dick and it scared the shit out of me. I tried to find out how it worked, and accidentally broke off the plastic stopper by fiddling around with it – so I shoved it back in the drawer and ran! Mum later asked if I had been snooping in her drawers, and of course I vehemently denied it like only an eight-year-old could. But, I soon learned, the world of sex toys had moved on a lot since then. Sure, you can still find massive dildos if that's what floats your boat, but I also discovered smaller, quieter, more high-tech toys that seemed less intimidating. At first, I bought one of those lipstick-sized vibrators you could store discreetly in your handbag and no one would know. I liked it – but it still wasn't enough to replace my wondrous hands.

Later on, I discovered one of those suction-style sex toys that uses air to imitate the sucking action of oral sex. Mine is the LELO Sona. Fuck. Me. That was game-changing, and was enough to stop me from using my fingers. You put it against your clitoris and suction pressure is applied. The first time I used it, my eyes opened wide, my expression startled, and I came in about 20 seconds. It was short, sharp and the orgasm was explosive. It has been my favourite toy ever since – I bloody love it. The worst thing is when you're having a great time and it suddenly dies – it's like someone has snatched your child out of your hands! The frenzy that ensues is slightly worrying.

But discovering masturbation didn't mean I gave up on partnered sex altogether. In fact, it was exactly the opposite: it helped me find my way back to sex again. The more comfortable I felt in touching myself, the more I felt like I could open up to my partner. As my confidence gradually increased, I finally felt ready to be vulnerable with him again. One evening, when we were both lying in bed, I told him all about my self-discovery and, although he was a little taken aback by my sudden need for a sex-toy drawer, he welcomed the change. The next time we had sex, I had the language to instruct him to do the same things I'd learned I liked, and our sex life improved massively as a result. I no longer felt ashamed for needing clitoral stimulation to accompany pene- tration, and he wasn't left fumbling in the woods, trying to find the best route. It was a win-win scenario. We started using vibrators during sex, which was fun and explorative. I'm not sure I would have had the confidence to initiate these new, seemingly scary, elements into the sex we had together had I not tried it all myself first. I know, now, that self-pleasure and self-love is not the antithesis to loving someone else – actually, it should be an integral part of the process. It might sound clichéd, but you do have to learn to love yourself first.

That said, there remains quite a substantial gap between female pleasure during masturbation, and during part- nered sex. In a TENGA survey from 2016, 30% of women said they found masturbation more pleasurable than having sex, compared to 21% of men. I'm sure this is because some women still feel uncomfortable sharing their learnings from masturbation with their partners. It could also be because masturbation feels like a low-pressure environment, where women aren't expected to perform and please others. You don't have to think about how the other person is feeling, or how your body is looking – you can just be. I get it: for many women, who are always expected to serve others, that can feel like such a relief. Though, I hope that, one day, we can all experience those feelings of sheer freedom and liberation from partnered sex just as much as we do from masturbation. In fact, I hope that, one day, we can feel that *all the fucking time*.

*

Over the past few years, I've gone through a huge shift in the way I view masturbation. I used to think it was the worst possible thing you can do, and now I talk about it openly and joyfully online – to tens of thousands of followers. I was even filmed having a wank (under the covers) for a Channel 5 documentary, called *How to Have a Better Orgasm*. You could say I'm a born-again masturbator. Now I have seen the light, I'm hell-bent on ensuring that women don't feel ashamed, or scared, of exploring their own bodies. It is such a natural, normal, healthy way to release tension and enjoy ourselves, and we all deserve that.

I don't always masturbate purely for the fun of it. Sometimes, I feel like I *need* it, for my health and well-being. If I masturbate when I'm in pain, with headaches or stomach cramps, it always makes me feel better. And it turns out, there's actually some scientific backing for that: it's believed that orgasms can help with pain relief because they release endorphins, which have pain-killing properties. But I think there's another benefit too: that the physical act of tending to myself and my body helps me to distract myself. I masturbate when I'm struggling to get to sleep, and this is proven to help too. When you pleasure yourself, you release oxytocin – the 'comfort hormone' – which calms your mind, and dopamine and serotonin, which leave you feeling satisfied; this all encourages better sleep.

Even when you don't reach orgasm (as this won't happen every time), I still believe it's a profound and brilliant method of self-care. It's a way of sitting with yourself, of getting in tune with your own body and sensations. It offers an opportunity to switch off from whatever anxious thoughts are threatening to consume you. Even if you have mind-blowing sex with a partner several times a week, I still think that taking the time to masturbate – to have pleasure on your own terms – is so valid and worthwhile. I know I'm not the only one. That same TENGA survey from 2019 found that 64% of people think masturbating is a form of self-care, while 90% said they felt it impacted their mood in some way.

When I was in a really terrible place, angry with my body for all the ways it had betrayed me, masturbation brought me back to myself. It got me back in touch with that girl who humped teddies, the girl who could self-soothe and follow her instincts. It made me realise I can be autonomous. It helped me believe that I am strong, and worthy. When I felt lost, I found myself through feeling myself.

Feeling Myself

When I asked my Instagram followers about their masturbation habits, 10% of you said you didn't masturbate at all, and 39% of you said you attach shame to masturbating. I hear you, loud and clear. When you've been told something is dirty or wrong or unimportant for so long, it's hard to rewrite the script. But I promise that when you untangle that bundle of confusion and self-hatred, it'll be liberating.

My advice? Start by scheduling some time in your diary that is just for you. Get into your most comfortable state – whether that's in your silkiest, prettiest pyjamas in bed, or in a piping-hot bath – and commit to feeling yourself. Don't start with the goal in mind to orgasm – just have a go at exploring. Stay curious, and feel for where the sensations feel more enjoyable. A little to the right, a little to the left, maybe a finger or two inside – see how you go. Try different things – tickle your nipples and maybe even touch your anus. Not working for you? That's absolutely fine – try something else. Dr Laurie Mintz recommends buying yourself a sex toy – perhaps a small, unintimidating vibrator that you can use against your clitoris – and using lubricant. Try watching (ethical) porn while you do it, or maybe read a sexy story. Picture fantasies in your head – don't worry if they seem weird or completely outside of the realm of what you'd want to try in real life. That doesn't matter at all – no one has a magnifying glass to look inside your brain, so let your thoughts run wild. And if it feels uncomfortable or scary the first time, keep coming back to it – normalising it will make it so much easier. And, eventually, I hope, you'll keep coming, and coming, and coming . . .

Masturbation

Female masturbation (alongside orgasms) is still not taught in sex education in schools, but seeing as the curriculum is already changing so much, I'm hopeful that it will be in future. Bring on the days when it'll be spoken about as openly and matter-of-factly as male masturbation. After all, I've recently learned that there's absolutely no reason why men should 'need' to wank more than women. The health benefits are very similar. The only reason this idea became common knowledge was because of the prevailing idea that men are simply unable to control their urges. But, in reality, they're able to control them just as much as women are. Anyone with a penis or a vagina should masturbate as frequently or infrequently as they please – in whatever way suits their lifestyles and their desires.

'Unless it's getting in the way of other things in your life, there's no such thing as masturbating too much,' Dr Karen Gurney told me – so, go forth and wank whenever you can.

Like with every part of sex, I talk to my pre-teen kids about masturbation. They often find my sex toys by the sink when I've been giving them a wash (hygiene is crucial), and they'll roll their eyes and moan about it, but I much prefer the openness than having them find them in my underwear drawer, wondering what the fuck they are. They know that, while there are so many things to be scared of out in the big bad world, their body parts, desires and sensations are absolutely nothing to be afraid of. I really wish more parents emphasised this with their kids. There's already enough to fear in life – masturbation shouldn't be added to the list. If anything, it's something we should celebrate. We can experience a kind of drug-like euphoria by rubbing a part of our bodies – isn't that just magical?!

In all honesty, every time I start masturbating, I can hear that tiny voice telling me that I'm doing something wrong, and unforgivable. But the voice is becoming fainter and fainter every time, and I'm learning to squash it altogether. Once again, I'm making a conscious, concerted effort to forgive myself for breathing in the toxic fumes of patriarchy. I forgive myself for buying into ideas that my morality is inter-twined with where on my body I put my fingers. Sometimes, I feel upset about all the years I wasted not knowing about the magic of masturbation, but I'm also glad I went on this journey, because it has taught me so much. It's a reminder that it's never too late to find yourself, to unlearn the things you thought you knew. Now, I will continue to question taboos and deep-held beliefs – always asking, why? Does this belief actually serve me? Is this true for me right now? Learning to feel myself physically has encouraged me to feel myself emotionally and mentally too – to look inward, rather than relying on other people and external factors. And the more we do that, the freer we become.

What I've learned about masturbation:

- You do not have to wait for permission from someone else to explore your body. It belongs to you and there is absolutely no shame in touching yourself as often as you like.

Masturbation

- Masturbation isn't just for single people – make time to masturbate even if you're in a long-term committed relationship and you have sex often. It's a completely different experience knowing you don't have to please anyone else, only yourself, and we should all make time for that.

- Plan for some time with yourself, in the same way you might plan any other sexual encounter. Wear nice lingerie, light some candles, put on a sexy playlist. It can be a self-care ritual as much as anything else.

- Try mixing up techniques. If you only use a vibrator, you might become over-reliant on this method and struggle to develop alternative pathways to pleasure. This isn't so great when you forget to charge your BFF!

- We have collectively created a culture of shame around female masturbation, and we can all work to unpack that. Initiate a conversation about it with your friends. Talk about it openly online. Speak to your children about it. The more we can talk openly, the more we can break the stigma and reduce the shame.

7

Marriage

Not so long ago, sex outside of marriage was considered the ultimate sin. In some cultures and communities, it still is. Throughout time, women who have had sex with men they weren't married to have had their reputations ruined (sometimes, they were even killed). It's complete insanity, but we live in a world where religious and patriarchal structures have decided that female sexuality is dirty and wrong – except during marriage. When a woman is married, sex is something different altogether; it's pure, clean and even holy, because she's fulfilling her duty of bearing children and serving her husband. The reasons for this used to be marginally rational (as a way of determining paternity) but mostly misogynistic and oppressive (as an assertion of ownership over women, and policing their natural desires). What a load of utter bollocks.

Thankfully, most of us don't live with that kind of expectation any more. In Britain, there was the swinging sixties, the arrival of the contraceptive pill, and the sexual revolution that helped us to evolve somewhat. But still, the fixation with marriage remains. We view it as the ultimate sign of success and social standing. We glorify it in songs, books, television shows and movies. Almost every story with a romantic plot line ends with a dramatic kiss and a hopelessly-in-love couple riding off into the sunset. We consider it to be the perfect happy ending. We obsess over celebrities' wedding pictures, and I've noticed that we congratulate people far more for getting engaged than we would if they got promoted. We praise people who manage to stay in long-lasting partnerships, and we look down on people who get divorced, or have lives filled with flings and short-lived relationships. Even though we might not say it, even though we think we've moved on, there's still an idea that sex inside a long-term committed relationship is worthy, beautiful and romantic. Anything that sits outside of that is a failure.

Unsurprisingly, while growing up I was obsessed with the idea of marriage. To me, it was the epitome of a stable, secure and happy life. I believed finding a man – and keeping him forever – would solve all my problems. I dreamed of the fairy-tale wedding, with the beautiful white dress, and a man who adored me whispering 'you look fucking amazing' when I reached him at the end of the aisle. I wanted to have a partner who worshipped the ground I walked on. I didn't even stop to consider what would come after that; what work and commitment lay beyond that initial exchanging of vows. I didn't even think that you could find happiness – and sexual freedom – in other ways.

*

Feeling Myself

I met the man who would become my husband when I was just 16 years old. He was walking up the stairs of the concourse at our sixth form college, and I craned my neck desperately trying to see the face of this bandy-legged boy who I was instantly attracted to – even though I'd never seen him before, and couldn't even see his face. This weird sense of knowing settled over me – as soon as I saw him, I knew I was going to marry him. I know what you're thinking: that's bullshit! That doesn't happen! This is what new friends would tell us, anyway, when we'd recount the story at 2am to anyone who would listen. But I promise you (and I promised them), I knew instantly. It was a warm, relaxed, happy feeling; an understanding that our coming together was inevitable. It was like a premonition. I didn't know any details but I knew there was a bigger story in my life that included him.

We met properly a few days later in the college's smoking area, a dingy concrete corner at the back of the building. A mutual friend introduced us.

'Alright,' he said, cigarette still dangling from his mouth as he gave me a hug. He was wearing a navy puffer jacket with red jeans and a bright-yellow jumper with YSL written huge on the front (don't you just love nineties fashion?). I had been wondering what his face looked like since I'd seen his back, and I was more than pleasantly surprised. To me, his face was perfect. He had beautiful blue eyes with long eyelashes, a strong nose and great bone structure. His eyes were red-rimmed and crusty from the rave he'd been to the night before, but that only seemed to add to his appeal. To top it off, he had dirty-blond hair shaped into a

Liam Gallagher haircut, which added to the whole edgy-boy look.

There was an air of cockiness about him that wasn't as natural as he probably liked to think. He was bouncing around with high energy, but I could sense some anxiety beneath the surface that he was trying to cover up by seeming funny and cool. He bragged about how wild he had been partying the night before – I knew he was showing off but I saw right through it. He loved the attention. He loved being the crazy one. Even at that age, I could tell that this came from a deep sense of wanting to be liked and needing to belong. I understood that, because I felt it too. It only made me like him more.

I observed him quietly. I interacted enough to be friendly, but not too much, as I didn't want him to know how enamoured I was. Afterwards, I couldn't stop thinking about him. And thankfully, that weekend, I was out with my friends at a bar (thanks to our fake IDs) when he walked in with a bunch of his mates. My heart fell to the floor. I pointed him out to my friends – they all thought he was rather attractive too. One of them jokingly suggested that we have a threesome. So, with confidence sponsored by snakebite (lager, cider and a dash of blackcurrant cordial), I walked up to where he was standing at the bar.

'Hello,' I said, tilting my head suggestively. 'One of my friends wants to have a threesome. You in?'

I thought this would be a pretty good bullshit filter. I never wanted to date a playboy. I'd seen my mum hurt by far too many men who loved themselves, and other women. I wanted to see if he was like the men I'd known, who couldn't be trusted. (Back then, I thought threesomes were the ultimate sign of promiscuity; the opposite of the stable, secure, loving relationship that I wanted. Little did I know that I was so preoccupied with them because, deep down, they were a fantasy of mine. I wouldn't admit that to myself until later, though). I dangled the bait in front of him, but he didn't take it.

'I'm not interested in any of your friends,' he replied, with a cheeky smile, and there was a bit of flirty banter back and forth. A few minutes later, one of my friends pulled me away (I didn't want to leave the conversation, but I was trying to play it cool) and when I went back to find him, I discovered that he'd gone. He'd fucking left! 'What a twat,' I thought.

But I wasn't giving up that easily. I encouraged my friends to down their drinks and leave, so we could head to another bar down the road in search of him. And thank god, he was there. I cornered him when he was coming back from the toilet and we snogged. It was unreal. So much so that I don't think we stopped kissing for the rest of our time at college. We drove our friends mad – there was a constant smacking of lips and squelching of saliva any time we were around. It was so unsociable but we couldn't help ourselves. I'd never felt magnetism like it. I've since realised that there is something in saliva that informs me whether I have a connection with a person or not. I had snogged quite a few boys up to that point and I'd known from the first kiss whether I liked them or not. Most were dumped straight after. Kissing is an incredible indicator for me – even with friends. If they're up for it, I try to have a snog with most people I like, even platonically. It either cements or annihilates a relationship. After all these tests, I like to think I've perfected my craft and I'm a very good kisser. Anyway, I digress.

We partied hard for those first few years after we got together, and we would spend hours in bed, bonding over the shitter parts of our childhoods. Now, I can see I was clearly filling a void left over from childhood trauma. I felt I'd met my person, and I adored everything about him. As in many young relationships, we didn't stop shagging. But unlike my first boyfriend, I didn't jump into bed because I felt like I had to – I actually wanted to have sex with him. We had the most amazing emotional connection, which physical intimacy only seemed to strengthen. I don't remember having orgasms in those early days but I thought it was incredible regardless. I think that the technicalities of sexual pleasure don't seem as important when you're having sex with someone who feels like your equal, your partner. Sleeping with someone you really like is a completely different experience. It could feel almost spiritual, as if we were two bodies joining together. But it could also just be fucking fun – especially when we were off our faces. Both of us could be shy and reserved in sex, but after getting in from all-night raves, we'd try every position known to man during hours of love-making. There were no inhibitions, and I'd often crave that kind of freedom when I was sober.

Our teen years were electric, but probably a bit co-dependent. We'd finish each other's sentences and we wanted to be around each other all the time. To be honest, I think I lost myself inside the relationship. I'm not sure I knew who I was, or what I wanted, if it wasn't somehow connected to him. Like me, he was broken in many ways – but, unlike a lot of the other men I'd known, he was also emotionally available. He was open about how he felt about me, and about his fears and struggles. I liked to reassure him, to calm him when he felt overwhelmed. I liked feeling needed.

For so many years, I'd watched my mum have disastrous relationships with men. I had been witness to her being raped, beaten up and treated as if she was disposable. I know none of that was her fault, but I was desperate to create the opposite kind of life for myself. I had made a conscious decision: my man would treat me with respect, he'd be kind, financially stable, supportive and, most importantly, he'd stick around.

But he had his own baggage too, and he was much more reticent about the idea of getting married. He was very open about not ever wanting to get married and, rather than letting our conflicting viewpoints deter me, I saw this as a challenge – and I set about wearing him down. I guess you could say I fell into the trap that so many women do, of thinking that I could 'fix' him. Later, in a workshop, I'd learn that I was fulfilling the role of 'rescuer'. But I'm also incredibly stubborn and determined when I get the bit between my teeth. I was adamant that he was the person I wanted to settle down with. I had an overwhelming desire to make people love me, and getting married was the most explicit symbol of this.

Alongside our love of partying and fun, we both knew we wanted to build successful lives for ourselves. He was ambitious, and was intent on climbing the career ladder. So much so that, when the opportunity to go travelling in our early twenties arose, he decided not to come with me, as he wanted to focus on work. I was devastated; I knew it would risk our relationship, but I didn't want a man to hold me back from doing something that I would regret later on (considering how much I valued love, I'm pretty impressed with my younger self for having this foresight). So I left him behind for nine months of backpacking with my friend. We spoke every day, exchanging sexy, flirty emails, talking about what we'd do to each other when we were finally reunited. He came out to visit me twice – once in Bali and once in Australia. I'd meet him at the airport, anxiously excited with a stomach full of butterflies. I think it made us only more determined to make it work.

Throughout our twenties, I probably would've told people that we had a great sex life. We still had sex regularly, but we fell into a routine of the same positions, normally in bed, before we went to sleep. I told myself it was satisfying enough, but I always craved something more exciting and novel, like threesomes or having sex in public. But I also felt ashamed of these desires, and thought I should be content with what I had. I didn't want to push him or seem like I was being 'too much', so I settled with being comfortable with the sex the way it was.

After all, sex didn't feel like the biggest, most all-encompassing part of our relationship. And this definitely isn't a bad thing: sex isn't the only form of intimacy you can have with another person. According to expert Emily Nagoski, legendary sex educator, researcher and author of

Come As You Are, 'different types of intimacy are created in different ways. They feel different, and they serve different purposes in a relationship.'

'Intimacy' is essentially just a feeling of closeness, of feeling known by someone. Physicality and sex is an important part of that equation – helping you release oxytocin, the comfort and bonding chemical – but there are many others, like talking, or even doing a hobby together. You can have sex without being truly intimate, and you can be beautifully intimate without having sex. So it's okay for other types of intimacy to take precedence, sometimes. In those early years, our emotional intimacy was incredible. Love, for us, was about supporting each other, through the tears and breakdowns in the middle of the night, and always being there on the other end of the phone. It was an exchange of needs – I was his supporter and comfort, and he was the stability of a male figure that I craved as a child. Even when our physical intimacy waned, we always had that to fall back on.

After travelling, I moved into his shared flat for a short while. I decided to train as a midwife and eventually we got our own little flat in London near the hospital I was working for. I felt so grown up buying plants to decorate the teeny tiny balcony that overlooked train tracks. The pressure on him to propose ramped up a million percent as I craved a change in the dynamic and wanted to move onto the next stage of our lives. One year, he suggested going to the local Thai restaurant for New Year's Eve instead of going out partying. I thought, 'well, this is new. He must be planning to propose to me at midnight.' So, I wore my best dress and highest heels, had my nails newly manicured and was nervously excited all day. Well, he didn't propose; he had no idea what I was thinking and was completely bamboozled when I spent the whole day of 1 January in bed crying hysterically. God, I'm so embarrassed looking back. It all comes down to our obsession with engagement – we've been taught that we need a ring on our finger to be truly loved. I can't be the only person who was absolutely fixated on it. And, sadly, that wasn't the only meltdown I had about him not proposing when I had got it into my head that he was going to.

When he eventually asked me to marry him after we'd been together for a decade, it was perfect. It was just after a sunset dinner for two while we were on holiday. He got down on one knee while my back was turned. I yelled, 'fuck off! You're joking, right?' It had been such a long time coming I thought it would never happen. In that moment, I felt like the luckiest person in the world. I'd always struggled with feeling accepted by family; growing up mixed-race, my grandparents had disowned my mother and me. I lacked belonging. So to have someone ask me, essentially, to become their family, I felt like I had found my home. His own family had been so kind, accepting me and welcoming me into their lives. I believed everything I had been taught: that this marriage would protect me. It would be pure and romantic and beautiful. Most of all, I believed that belonging to him would give me the sense of peace I had been searching for since childhood.

But on the morning of our wedding day, a lavish party I had visualised since childhood, I felt incredibly anxious. It was the loneliest I had ever felt. Looking back, I think some part of me, deep down, knew it wasn't right. I think I knew that ultimately my unresolved issues of needing to be unconditionally loved – left by my absent father – couldn't be satiated by romantic love, no matter how much the other person tried. I think I must've known that I was just following the path laid out for me, without questioning whether it was really the right direction for me. I didn't tell anyone about how I was feeling, shunning friends and family and spending the morning alone. I felt I should be grateful. This amazing man wanted me. Me! I couldn't understand why I was feeling so lonely. Wasn't I marrying my best friend? Eventually, though, I brushed my fears aside and walked down that aisle and I had the most wonderful day. We partied long into the night and I had the best time dancing on tables and singing along to 'In Love' by Chase and Status (on repeat – it became the soundtrack to our wedding). When my groom carried me to bed while I was still in my wedding dress, as the morning workers arrived for their shift, it was just how I'd always pictured it. All the morning's fears had dissipated. This was what I wanted. Finally, I felt like I wasn't yearning any more. I was happy.

Unfortunately, though, that feeling I had on my wedding morning would creep up to bite me on the bum later on.

*

Unsurprisingly, sex declined down quite a steep cliff when we had our kids – our eldest was born in 2009, after our engagement but before we got married, and our youngest was born in 2012, a year after we tied the knot. I've already talked about the toll early motherhood took on my body image, but there were a whole host of other issues to contend with – we were no longer those free teenagers who could spend hours partying and love-making while we figured out what we wanted from life. No, being in an adult long-term relationship was a whole different ball game. There was work, and kids, and financial responsibilities, and trying to keep up with our families – and all this meant we were, frankly, exhausted most of the time.

I often felt a lot of pressure to sustain sexual intimacy. I thought that if I didn't have sex with my husband, he would lose interest in me and I'd be kicked to the kerb. I'd speak to friends about how often they were having sex, and I'd feel nervous about the fact we weren't having it as much as we should.

Sometimes – like when I was suffering with body image issues – I know our dry spells were caused by me. But other times, my libido would be higher, and he would pull back, and I'd complain that I didn't feel wanted or desired. During these times, I'd try to initiate sex more – often, I just wanted to feel close to him; to feel wanted and needed. I read a magazine article about a woman who committed to having sex every single day for a whole month, which I suggested we try, but we couldn't make it stick. I also got annoyed that I was the one initiating sexual intimacy all the time, and I began to feel rejected and disillusioned, which led me to retreat further.

I've since learned that there's no 'perfect' quantity to have sex with a partner. 'Normal is whatever you both are comfortable with,' wrote legendary relationship therapists

John Gottman and Julie Schwartz Gottman in their book, *Eight Dates*. 'Normal will change often throughout the life of your relationship – as you have children, as you age, as you deal with medical issues. It's all a normal part of human sexuality, and it's all okay.'

In fact, we should actively expect sex to fall off the table: scientists say that the passion you feel when you're falling in love lasts two or three years at most.

'When you first meet someone, there's this dopamine rush and adrenaline kicks in as you're trying to find out more,' sex and relationship therapist Charlene Douglas (who you may recognise from *Married at First Sight UK*) told me. 'But once you get to know each other, there's no mystery any more. You know the good and bad, and all the unsexy things come into a relationship, like who will put out rubbish and feed the children, which has an impact on sexiness, desire and passion.'

In a *Cosmopolitan* survey from 2017, which polled 1,162 married participants from ages 20–29, they found that 52% of married people wished they had more sex. And they discovered that the sex they had declined, too – 24% of respondents said they had sex four or more times a week before marriage (a hefty amount, if you ask me) but only 9% had sex so frequently after marriage.

I've since learned that a depletion of sex, in its own right, isn't something to worry about. When I spoke to sex expert Emily Nagoski, she told me that it's 'inevitable' to go through ups and downs of desire. 'If a relationship lasts long enough, there will be a constant ebb and flow of sexual connection,' she said. 'It will definitely happen.'

Sometimes, you want to have sex anywhere, any place, and, other times, the thought of even touching your partner makes you want to hurl. There are a huge range of factors that determine why this is – from our hormones, to how stressed we are. But the problem is that physical intimacy and emotional intimacy are intertwined. So, often, when you're not connecting physically, the emotional distance between you grows too.

I noticed cracks showing when it wasn't just the sex that was declining, but other forms of physical intimacy too. The kissing, that always signified a deeper closeness for me, became rare and fleeting. Pecks on the cheek, as we said hello and goodbye, replaced full-blown snogs. At night-time, instead of clambering over each other, we'd collapse into separate sides of the bed, craving sleep more than each other's touch.

I didn't know it at the time, but we were speaking completely different love languages. Coined by American pastor and author Dr Gary Chapman, the five love languages are essentially the different ways we like to give and receive love – and when you don't learn to consciously speak your partner's love language, this is when you run into trouble. I craved physical touch – I needed my hand held or my feet stroked in order to feel loved. But his love language was 'acts of service' – he was showing his love to me by going out to work, looking after me and building the life we had dreamed of. We weren't speaking each other's languages, which made us both feel unloved and under-appreciated. I highly recommend finding out what your love languages are – you can find the quiz online at

5lovelanguages.com. Teaching yours to your partner, and learning theirs, is such an essential way of ensuring you're on the same emotional page. I wish I knew about it before.

Gradually, the emotional intimacy that we had always prided ourselves on started blurring out of focus, and I felt bereft. I always thought I could cope with barely any sex, but what I couldn't cope with was not feeling wanted. After working on my body issues following having my children, I started feeling empowered and sexy, my career was flying high and I felt I was growing and smashing most areas of my life – except my relationship. I wanted someone who would come up behind me, grab my hips and kiss me on the neck, or even say goodnight and cuddle me tightly in bed before we drifted off. But that wasn't happening.

And I know a big part of this problem was that I wasn't communicating how I felt with my husband. 'Within relationships, lots of key conversations stop being had, and they're replaced by assumption,' Charlene told me. I assumed that, because I wasn't getting what I wanted, I wasn't loved or desired. It made me feel lost and disconnected.

There are so many different issues we can come up against over the course of a long-term relationship. Worrying that we are too horny, or not horny enough. Feeling like the sex we're having isn't satisfactory. Feeling like we're expected to have sex too much. Feeling unsexy or undesirable. You've probably felt one (or all) of these things over the course of a relationship, and I bet you've squashed those feelings and tried to pretend they didn't exist. I know I have. But, news flash: pretty much all of these problems can be solved by a good old-fashioned chat.

Marriage

As Dr Laurie Mintz already mentioned, it's important to have these conversations outside of the bedroom – and Charlene Douglas agreed. 'Often couples raise issues during the height of passion, and if you say you're not enjoying how things are, that can cause resentment and a lack of sexual drive.'

So, pick a night to crack open a bottle of wine and just talk about sex. Keep it light and fun, discussing what you like and don't like, how your levels of desire have changed over the course of your relationship, what you want to prioritise from that point onwards. And, advises Charlene, it's also vital to prioritise your emotional connection too.

'Make time every day – just twenty or thirty minutes – where you actually talk and connect,' she says, because we know just how important emotional intimacy is.

Ultimately, it does take a lot of work to maintain erotic connection in a long-term relationship, and a lot of us just wander through our relationships with our eyes closed, hoping that the burning flame of love is enough to see us through. Now, I know that it just isn't. It doesn't matter how in-love you are, the flame is always going to dim somewhat. You have to be really intentional and conscious about adding logs to the fire and keeping it going, even when it feels fucking hard.

You might want to try new things to spice up your sex life, but remember that the focus should always be on pleasure and enjoyment – not just what you *think* couples should do. So if butt play or threesomes weren't ever something you'd considered before, it's unlikely doing one of these things is going to solve all your problems.

'The body doesn't lie,' Charlene said. 'If your brain and body don't feel comfortable with something, then you might have issues with the sexual arousal process and you could struggle to orgasm.'

Emily Nagoski agrees. 'Pleasure is the measure,' she often says, and it's a phrase I try to remind myself of. ' "Pleasure is the measure" of sexual well-being, not how much you crave it, not how often you have, or with whom or why or where or how many orgasms you have. If you *like* the sex you are having, you are doing it right. The rest is just finding your way to a state of mind where pleasure is possible.'

And this is where the talking becomes so important – we all have different desires and fantasies; different things that get us going. But trying to do something just to please your partner is unlikely to end well for you. Sure, we've been led to believe that sex is something you 'have' to do to sustain a relationship, but it's also something you should want to do, for yourself. So you can feel good. And if you're only doing sexual acts to satisfy a partner, you're going to end up having very few orgasms (not ideal), and you may find resentment clogging up inside the cracks of your relationship and causing more issues later down the line. It's simply not worth it.

My husband and I did eventually emerge from our sexual funk: sex toys, and opening ourselves up to learning together, helped. But sadly our emotional intimacy had waned, and sex isn't the only thing that can keep a relationship afloat.

*

Marriage

We had many challenges during our marriage. Sometimes, we would come together like a team and other times, these difficulties would push us further apart. Dealing with challenges differently is, of course, very normal in any relationship. We all have varying fight-or-flight responses and we confront hurt in different ways. But the problem came when we stopped communicating and became increasingly detached.

I think the sexiest thing in the world is to feel seen and heard – but I started to feel the opposite. I felt like I was in a dark room, mouth as wide as it would go, trying to scream, but no sound would come out. There's a famous painting by Edvard Munch called *The Scream* that depicts a ghost-like figure, mouth stretched wide into a black hole. That was me. That's how I felt, day in and day out, in my marriage. The pain was palpable and I was trying to get the sound out and be heard, but no matter what I tried it wasn't happening. Paradoxically, I felt I was being listened to and taken seriously outside of the home. I sought solace in my phone as my Instagram profile rose, the validation from strangers temporarily patching over my broken heart. My career had rocketed and I was really proud of myself; I was doing shoots with high street brands one day and being asked to talk on panels the next. I was writing articles about my experiences, collaborating with huge brands, even designing my own pair of shoes with Marks and Spencer, which sold out in hours. On the outside, it looked like I was smashing it – and I was – but mostly it took me away from what was going on at home. I felt like I had handed over my life bringing up our children when they were young, supporting my husband's career as he rose, and now it was my time to revel in this new and exciting opportunity that I had built from nothing. He said he was proud of me, but our lives felt like they were going in different directions, and I wasn't receiving that validation from where I wanted it most: my marriage and my person.

Eventually, we decided to go to counselling to discuss the breakdown of communication, which really helped us to talk to each other without screaming, and attempt to understand the patterns we were repeating. I would recommend couples' counselling to everyone, if it's financially viable. Just abandon the shame of thinking you've 'failed' and prioritise understanding your partner. Because that's fundamentally what it does. Being in a relationship can often feel like a cloudy bubble; it can be hard to make sense of situations, and see them clearly, while you're inside them. I used to feel like my head was about to explode because I just didn't understand why I was reacting the way I was, or why he couldn't see my point of view. Therapy helped us to see each other's perspectives, rationally and coherently. It certainly isn't the place you go to get someone else to agree with you, and help you gang up against your partner. It's also not somewhere you can drop off your partner to be fixed (as I quickly realised), but is a lot about understanding your own role in the relationship. I learned to accept and acknowledge that we all fuck up, we make poor choices, react badly and say and do stupid, hurtful things, but that doesn't make us bad people. It makes us human. We had some incredible ah-ha moments during therapy, where the penny would drop and the whole situation would become clearer. We also had some painfully awkward, brutal moments where all I wanted to do was jump on a plane to Mexico and never come back. But we stuck with it, and worked hard to bandage up the wounds we'd both caused.

Ultimately, I think our commitment to therapy is why we remain good friends after we eventually decided to separate in 2020. We couldn't align our differences enough to make it work – we had both changed too much; we wanted, and needed, different things from our lives. But we have so much respect for one another, and we know neither of us are nasty or evil. And, despite our differences, we are united in the common goal of wanting to do the best for our children. We want to improve on our own upbringings – and that will always unite us.

*

I used to think that the breakdown of a marriage was a colossal failure. Something to be ashamed of. My biggest goal in life was to find someone who would stay. I thought that finding my person – and keeping him – would make my life complete. Spoiler: it didn't. I walked through life not questioning whether I should want a boyfriend, to get engaged, to get married, to buy a house, to have children. I just followed the path with my eyes closed, and hoped I would reach paradise. There was no critical thinking going on – I didn't question anything, examining why I was making the choices I was. I didn't question the fact I had gobbled up idealised visions of what marriage involved.

That said, I don't regret the decades I spent with him. There were times of long nights and fun sex; there was security and joy, among periods of chaos and disillusionment. We became grown-ups, and parents, as a team. It wasn't always happy and beautiful, but it will always be a part of me and I'm grateful for the love we shared. My life had been stained by the actions of men, but he was the first man I could trust and feel truly comfortable around, and I will always have love for him. I grew and learned so much about myself within that relationship. Now, I'm so much more sure about my wants and needs, how to communicate them and what I want my life (and love) to look like. Now the end of our relationship isn't quite so raw, I see my marriage as a huge triumph, despite not having had any great template to work from.

Despite all its difficulties, romantic love is still very important to me, and I still believe it's a valuable building block for good sex. My husband was the first person I enjoyed sex with, and I know that was down to the perfect combination of chemistry and feeling completely comfortable. The safety of being in a long-term committed relationship can help you feel completely vulnerable and surrender to pleasure and intimacy, there's no denying that. But I also know that romantic love can be a hindrance to sexuality too. When a relationship lasts a long time, it's so easy to fall into routines and the stress of everyday life takes over. Suddenly, sex can become something you have to do, rather than something you want to do, which can suck the life out of it. Renowned relationship therapist Esther Perel said something about this that really resonated with me, in

Marriage

The Sex Issue, a book compiled by Goop: 'Once a relationship becomes institutionalised (or formal, or legal), women often no longer feel in control. *Now she is married; here is what she is expected to do; this is what the world wants from her.* The moment a woman feels she has to do something that used to be a choice, that she felt owned ... it becomes a duty and not a pleasure. She loses her autonomous will, which is essential to desire.'

I think there's a lot of truth in that. Sex with someone you love can be a blessing, then a curse. But it doesn't have to be that way: the secret is to keep your eyes open to the challenges, acknowledge that they will come up (instead of walking around with rose-tinted glasses on, like I did), keep working at it, keep talking, and never be ashamed of seeking professional help as soon as cracks begin to show. Our closest relationships take up so much of our time, and space in our heads and hearts. I think they're worth investing in.

I'm much more clear-eyed about romantic love now. I know that it isn't the only goal in life we should strive towards. If I could go back and talk to my younger self, I'd tell her that love can't fill a hole in your life. It won't solve all your problems. It's unrealistic to pile so much expectation onto one person for fulfilling all of your needs. That's an impossible standard that they are bound to fall short of. And when you channel everything you have into one relationship, you start to lose yourself, which leads to resentment and disillusionment. I realise now that I was craving the love and attention that was lacking from my childhood, especially from the men in my life. But an adult relationship is different; love is conditional – it relies on mutuality and negotiation – unlike the unconditional love that a parent gives a child. Essentially, I was yearning for something that was impossible to fulfil.

Life won't always follow a pre-destined path; sometimes, we have to go off course in order to find ourselves. My marriage was a part of my journey, but it wasn't the perfect sunset at the end of the road, like I thought it would be. I'm slowly learning that nothing ever is. All we can do is keep on walking, challenging ourselves to grow and shapeshift along the way. Despite what we've been repeatedly taught, I've learned that long-term romantic love isn't the purest, holiest, most valuable kind. I've realised that a partner can't make you whole, or fill a crater opened up during childhood. Only you can do that. So whether we find that one person or not, what's most important is that we have everything we need to fill our own cups instead.

What I've learned about long-term relationships and marriage:

- Marriage is tough; it requires constant work. Love isn't something you have, it's something you do. Both people have to be really committed to being curious about one another as you grow and change, otherwise it stagnates. Set aside time to have date nights and proper, deep conversations. If you're not sure what kinds of questions to ask, *Eight Dates* by John Gottman and Julie Schwartz Gottman is a great place to start.

Marriage

- Alongside togetherness, separateness is also key for a strong relationship. Knowing you are an independent person, with your own likes, needs and interests separate from your partner, is so important. Having time to develop that relationship with yourself is essential.

- Don't walk through your relationship with your eyes closed, hoping it all works out. Be intentional about learning more about relationships, growing and changing. I recommend any book by psychotherapist Esther Perel; her podcast, 'Where Should We Begin?' is also great. *The 5 Love Languages* by Dr Gary Chapman will probably change your life too.

- Never be ashamed to seek couples' counselling if your communication is breaking down. Having an objective outside perspective can be hugely beneficial to help you both see things clearly.

- Understand that everyone is doing the best they can – judging the other person by focusing on their faults is very easy to do, but what's much harder is to look at what role you play in the dynamic of your relationship.

- Sex will require a bit more effort when you're in a relationship, and that's okay. Planning sex doesn't have to remove the spontaneity – the anticipation can be just as sexy as the main event.

Feeling Myself

- Never let your partner force you into doing things you're not comfortable with. This will only lead to resentment – and even trauma – further down the line. Communicate openly and honestly about your boundaries when it comes to sex. Just because you're in a relationship with someone doesn't mean you owe them anything.

8

Motherhood

Watching your child drink that last sip of water when you feel like you're dying of thirst on a scorching hot day, and being okay with it – that, in a nutshell, is motherhood.

But before I get into the highs and lows of being a parent, and how it ultimately helped unravel so much of my shame towards sex, I want to acknowledge all those who can't, or don't want to, have children. I completely understand that it might be painful (or boring!) to read about my experience of motherhood. If you are a parent, you may also find this chapter triggering as it details birth trauma, and touches on postnatal depression. Please feel free to skip this chapter – we all must do whatever we can to protect our hearts (and sanity).

Becoming a mother was something I always wanted, from a very young age. I wanted to give and receive love, unconditionally, in a way that couldn't quite be fulfilled or replicated with romantic love. Oh god, how I romanticised being a parent! I thought I'd never be a parent like mine. I would be loving, patient and kind. I would hold my child close to me as they rested their sleeping head on my chest and breathe in their intoxicating child smell. I would play with them all day long. I would cook food only from fresh (using organic ingredients). I would sit on the floor in their bedroom and make up fairy tales, reading them endless stories while their eyes drooped. Suffice to say, I had an extremely idealised version of motherhood in my head.

It's unsurprising, really. Our society has created an idea that mothers are angelic, perfect beings, generously martyring themselves for the good of their children and families. I mean, up until the last century, child-bearing was considered a woman's only purpose in life. Sex, for women, existed purely for creating lovely little humans. Throughout history, women have been expected to raise their sons to be strong, upstanding men, and raise their daughters to be just like them: quiet, timid, obedient. And, in the midst of all this, mothers are completely stripped of their identities as people. Sure, motherhood isn't the only expectation placed on women these days, but I think this idea does live on. Suddenly, women aren't free-thinking and independent any more. They exist in service to their offspring. Their attractiveness and sexuality, apparently, disappears as soon as they've popped a baby out of their vagina. Poof. Gone. If being sexual is not something 'good girls' should do, it's certainly not something 'good mothers' should do. Pleasure for pleasure's sake, and giving yourself wholly and completely to your child, seem incompatible.

Yep, I internalised all these ridiculous ideas. Before I even got pregnant, I knew I wanted to be that 'good mother'. I'd see those embarrassed parents in supermarkets, who would battle with their child as they lay on the floor, screaming, and I would judge them. I thought: how can they not see what the issue is? Why aren't they just giving their child the love they're craving? Or: why aren't they ignoring the bad behaviour? I always thought I knew the answer. I judged, too, when I saw children who spoke to their parents like crap, demanding things or not saying 'please' or 'thank you'. I was a pseudo-child psychologist before I was a parent. I strongly believed I wouldn't be a shit mother, like these other women were. I would know my child; they would listen to me, laugh with me, be my best friend and learn from me. It would be totally idyllic.

What a load of shite. I'm actually laughing out loud as I write this. What an absolute gold-medal tool I was! In fact, just now, my eldest child told me to shut up while I was helping her look for her fucking swimming costume after I offered to take her fucking swimming (because I try to be a good fucking parent). Yes, she just shouted at me to leave her room and swiftly slammed her door in my jaw-dropped face. One thing's for sure: I am definitely not the epitome of that calm, earthy, amazing mother I thought I would be. Honestly, I'd love to know how anyone manages it.

I had my first child when I was 29 and, after she was born, I thought I might never be able to have sex again. I believed that childbirth had – literally – broken me. For starters, the birth was traumatising. After over 24 hours of labouring naturally in a pool in a birth centre, I was taken for an emergency C-section. It was surreal to be taken to the nearest hospital – where I happened to work – via a flashing blue-light ambulance. Oh, the shame. I came through the doors on the stretcher, writhing, screaming and swearing very loudly. All I knew was that the pain was too much. I couldn't cope any more. It was time to get an epidural.

After receiving pain relief, I was allowed to labour more while they monitored her heartbeat with a CTG machine attached to my stomach. Her heartbeat kept dipping with each contraction – which I knew from my own work isn't completely uncommon, so the midwives weren't too concerned. Eventually, though, her heartbeat became increasingly concerning and they had to call the doctor from wherever he was sleeping to come and get my baby out, stat. When our daughter eventually came, she wasn't breathing, she had to be resuscitated and headed straight off to intensive care. My husband was frantic with worry and I was just so bloody bamboozled with everything that I was mostly catatonic except when I shouted 'what is happening, why isn't she crying?' and no one answered because they were busy giving her oxygen.

I didn't ever consider what impact the birth would have on me and my relationship. My husband would become emotional every time he recounted the story, telling people how traumatising it was and how terrified he was for both of us, but I played it down. I was a midwife; I'd seen these things happen before. I'd seen many emergencies during my work hours; it wasn't that unusual. I rationalised it. But just because something is normal doesn't mean it's any less traumatic. According to the Birth Trauma Association, around 30,000 women a year experience birth trauma in the UK. This can be caused by so many things: maybe, like mine, your baby's heartbeat dipped, or maybe you were rushed into an operating room for an emergency caesarean. Birth is fucking scary stuff, and we're lucky it's as safe as it is today, thanks to antibiotics and fantastic healthcare. That wasn't always the case: up until 1935, the mortality rate during childbirth was between 4 and 5 per 1,000 women. Today, it's a tiny fraction of that. Now, we're highly likely to survive birth, but so many of us are left with scars from psychological trauma. At that point, I was still adept at shutting out trauma. I know better now.

While I pushed down the trauma from my birth, I was also having to adapt to a completely new lifestyle. One incredibly naive thing to say before you have children is: A child won't change us. We're planning on the baby slotting into *our* lives. The baby will have to work around our schedule. We are still going to do all the eating out, nights out, all the travelling, all the sex ... everything will basically be like it was before, except we'll have this bundle of gurgling joy next us to complete our little love nest. Surely a baby isn't like that tornado everyone preaches about? Surely they're just trying to scare the bejesus out of us? 'Why do they have to be so dramatic?' I thought. 'It can't be that bad.'

Well, I had one part right. It's not like a tornado. It's a motherfucking apocalypse. If you're thinking about having kids, I want to tell you this: never, ever underestimate the monumental impact a baby will have on your lives, and then you might be a tiny teeny bit prepared for the change that's about to come. I'm sure you'll know by now that I don't sugar-coat things, and I'm not going to apologise nor qualify what I say about those early days and weeks of motherhood with, 'oh but there was good stuff too and we loved her so much'. Of course there were, and we did, but we hear about the beauty of motherhood all the time. Admitting the hard, gory and scary parts – not so much. We think it's shameful to admit that it's not all rainbows and butterflies. What I wish someone had told me, and what I want to tell you about now, is the brutal, harsh reality of how becoming a mother changed me and affected my relationship, especially our sex life. Are you ready? Okay, here we go.

First, there were the changes to my body that I have spoken about in Chapter 5, 'Bodies'. I hated what I saw. 'Devastated' is probably a more accurate term. I hadn't considered that my body would change completely – that there would be stretch marks, excess skin and weight gain. The change in shape. The loss of identity. I didn't understand how much of my self-worth was tied up in my appearance until after I became a mother. And I didn't even think about it affecting the sex we had. I remember thinking: this kid has fucked up my sex life, I'm never going to enjoy sex ever again – wow, what a sacrifice. I waited my whole life for this? I feel pretty bad describing it that way, but fuck it – that was my truth. That was honestly how I felt at the time. I think we've all had dark thoughts like this, and it's okay to admit that.

During those long drawn-out days of early motherhood, I was breastfeeding, and my daughter would wake every two hours to feed in the night. I was determined that my husband would not be moving from our bed into another room to get sleep just because he had work in the morning. He would hear the pain and the suffering. And also, I was adamant that a baby wouldn't change us. I was scared about sleeping in separate beds; I worried that too much distance would creep in between us. Instead, I moved our baby out of our room earlier than most to try to gain back some control over our exhausted, nappy-filled lives. I wanted to try to get out of the habit of picking her up at the slightest whimper, and get her out of the two-hourly waking pattern she had gotten into. In reality, it just meant I had to traipse down the corridor, half-asleep with my leaky bigger-than-your-head boobs and mahoosive pants a few times a night. Not quite the miracle solution I had hoped for. In trying to regain my sanity (and intimacy with my husband), I just ended up sacrificing myself more in the process. We do that all the time, don't we? We think we're doing what's right for our kids and our relationships, but we end up fucking ourselves over royally, and we become resentful. But 'good mothers' don't show their resentment. 'Good mothers' get on with it.

The overwhelming feeling of early motherhood was exhaustion. I was tired, so very tired, and I wondered why my baby was the only baby in the history of the world who didn't sleep. When I went to my local parent and baby group, the other parents told their smug tales about their babies sleeping for 11 hours straight. It made me want to puke and cry, possibly at the same time. I remember crying to my husband about how everyone else's children were so good. 'Why were we so unlucky?' I thought. But I've since realised that people lie, or they hide the truth with smiles.

Really, everyone was struggling in some small way – we all just have different methods of dealing with it. And, for some people, that means concealing how hard it really is.

And I know this, because I also pretended I was fine. I told everyone I was thrilled and they told me I was glowing, but in reality, I was terribly lonely. My baby had colic and she cried all the time. This meant I was exceptionally anxious to go out in public with her. She screamed so loudly, and it cut through me like a knife on room temperature butter. I cannot tell you the heart-plummeting feeling I felt when she cried – it still gives me shivers when I think about it now. If she'd wail in public or during the middle of the night, my whole body would stiffen and go cold. I was struggling to cope. I felt like I didn't know who I was any more without the background noise of a mooing cow (otherwise known as a breast pump).

I was also angry, and I struggled to contain my resentment. I felt like my husband's life hadn't changed much at all. He was still going out to work every day, attending his colleagues' leaving drinks or celebrating someone's birthday with yet more drinks. I was even jealous when he walked out the door to go to work at 5.30am even though I knew his work was anything but cosy. It was surely better than this. I felt like my life had done a 360 flip, and I just wasn't prepared for it. I waited desperately to hear that key in the door, and I tried with every fibre of my body to avoid jumping up, running to the door and breaking down on the floor by his feet. I tried to not throw the baby at him; to not scream. Instead I'd pretend that I had it together; I was chilled, relaxed (if a little tired) and, most importantly, I had this 'mothering' thing down. I'd usually be cooking dinner with one hand, rocking my crying daughter in the other, while trying to tackle the pile of washing that the laundry basket was struggling to contain. I knew exactly how that laundry basket felt.

The expectation placed on me, as her mother, felt immense. It felt like he could just drop in and drop out, changing the odd nappy and rocking her to sleep on the days when he wasn't at work. This is quite a common story. Even though we say, in theory, that women are equal to men, when it comes to parenting that just doesn't always translate. For starters, men still aren't eligible for the same parental leave rights as women – men are entitled to up to two weeks of paternity leave in the UK, while women's maternity leave can be a whole year. Yes, women give birth and (may) breastfeed their babies, but fathers are equally responsible in creating them, and should be offered the same opportunities to be a primary parent and take on that domestic role. I think that's the only way we'll achieve true equality. But with the laws as they currently are, it makes less sense for dads to take time off to take on the lion's share of raising their kids, not to mention the fact men's earning power still often outstrips women's. Plus, society's stereotypes and expect-ations also mean there's still a stigma about breadwinning mothers and stay-at-home dads. As with so many other couples, we had no choice: I had to be her primary parent. Thankfully, there are so many people (including my bril-liant friend Anna Whitehouse, aka Mother Pukka) who are campaigning to change this, so we can achieve true equality in parenthood. Until then, though, I think we will always come up against these challenges.

So many conflicting feelings rattled around inside my brain. Wasn't this what I had always wanted? I was a midwife, for crying out loud! I had been like a second parent to my siblings, twins born when I was 14 to my single mum. And even more than that: I was a woman. Surely I was built for this job? I knew I should be a fucking natural, but I felt like I was failing, all the time. And I was too afraid to tell anyone about it, because that would make it feel too real. Instead, I pretended, as best I could, that I was that perfect mother I had always dreamed of becoming.

Four weeks after giving birth, I convinced myself that I should have sex again. My self-hatred was spiralling, and I thought that perhaps my husband would be able to fuck some sense back into me and bring my old fun-loving spirit back into my body. I was also afraid of what might happen if we went for too long a period of not having sex; I'd grown up believing the horror stories of men leaving women who would no longer satisfy them, who prioritised their role as a mother above their role as a sexual being, and I didn't want to jeopardise our relationship. I still thought my old life was within reach. So, one day, when our daughter was napping in the next room, I decided to initiate sex. He was hesitant but went along with it. I tentatively raised my legs, despite the pain in my lower abdomen from the surgery only a few weeks earlier, in the hopes that the old me was down there somewhere.

I mean, what was I thinking? I was adamant that it was the right thing to do, but I wasn't physically, emotionally or mentally prepared. It felt terrible. I was scared. I was nervous that it would be painful – it wasn't as bad as I thought it might be in terms of the physical pain, but I wasn't present. Why did I pressure myself to rush this? From what I can remember (and, to be honest, it's not a lot from that time), I made all the right noises, pretended to enjoy it and that nothing much had changed, but I wasn't in the same postcode, let alone the same room. It felt different. Very bloody different. It was like my body was no longer mine. I was numb. I felt like a corpse. What had happened to my body? Was it even mine any more?

Now I know it's hardly surprising that I felt that way. Besides the physical element of vaginal tissue becoming thinner and drier, our bodies go through a whole load of hormonal changes after birth that can make sex feel less enjoyable.

'The hormones needed to breastfeed can reduce desire, so if you're breastfeeding, that can be an issue,' Dr Karen Gurney told me. 'Then there's things like tiredness, stress, adjusting to a new role, plus recovering from birth, birth injury and not feeling completely at home with your body yet. So, being distracted by things like leaky nipples, the change of body image, or whatever it might be. It's usually the psychological factors that can make sex feel less enjoyable for women after they've had a baby.'

According to sex and relationship therapist Charlene Douglas, sex in heterosexual relationships (where your partner is the father) can be strained because we subconsciously blame them for the pain of childbirth, and the issues we're experiencing.

'You might know your partner didn't mean to hurt you, consciously, but actually it's their sperm that contributed to all that you're going through,' she said, and I'm sure I felt that on some deep level. Plus, she explained, it's hard (particularly with penetrative sex) for your mind to reassociate your birth canal with something sexy, rather than pushing a baby out. 'The brain and body has to become used to another foreign object in the vagina and has to recognise it as pleasure, and that can take some time,' she said.

I mean, there's also simply the fact you're suddenly adapting to having a new screaming, demanding human to look after. It makes me laugh, really, to think I ever believed I'd be able to bounce back that easily. I'm sure some people do, but it's definitely not one universal experience for everyone. If you felt uncomfortable and detached from sex after having babies too, you're not alone.

Anyway, I learned the hard way. After that first far-too-soon sexual encounter with my husband, sex didn't happen again for a quite a long time. I was exhausted. He was exhausted. We had no energy to even have sexy thoughts let alone action them. I was still wearing my Primark multi-pack maternity pants for a good year after her birth and crying as I looked into the mirror at my dishevelled body. Sex was relegated to a division no one had ever heard of. In fact, most forms of physical touch got put on the back-burner. Our closeness became a distant memory. It's no wonder I struggled to come, even when I started to mastur-bate during those rare moments of quiet when our baby was napping during the day. It must have been the worst possible environmental conditions for pleasure. Much of the time, I felt like I wasn't attached to my body any more. I was completely lost.

*

It took a good two years before I started finding myself again. Gradually, I began to claw my way out of the deep, dark well I had found myself in. I could see the light at the top and I was inching towards it day by day, pulling up my whole (heavier) weight as I went. That weight was both literal and metaphorical. I was adjusting to the huge load of expectation about what a mother should be. I became that woman in the supermarket, unable to control her child, and warding off dirty looks from the passers-by. Opinions flew in like heat-seeking missiles that would land with a thump on my lap. 'Don't pick the baby up straight away when they cry.' 'Make sure you don't let them sleep on you.' 'Make sure the baby is facing this way.' 'Don't carry the baby like that.' Do this, don't do that ... It felt like everyone had an opinion, and I felt shackled by the new position and responsibility. That judgement I would cast on women before I had kids? Once I became a mother, I was the object of it, and I felt it deeply. Our culture has a big problem with judging and shaming women; we're constantly made to feel like we're not getting it right, and there's just no winning. We're never the right amount of pure and sexy. We're never the right amount of curvy and skinny. We're never able to find the sweet-spot of perfect motherhood, where we get everything right the first time. It's all so hard, and yet we allow absolutely no room for error.

Feeling Myself

The pressure to be a 'perfect' mother made me want to run away to the middle of the jungle where my baby and I would eat leaves and bathe in the stream, leaving all those pricks and their finger-pointing far behind. I just couldn't get my head around the fact that it all seemed to land at my feet and not my husband's. He only had to pick up our daughter, and he was heralded as Dad of the Year. People would coo and praise him for doing the bare minimum. I know it wasn't his fault the world acted this way – we're not used to seeing men as caring figures, so it feels unusual and therefore it's praised so much more. But it felt fucking unfair and I battled with it internally every day.

Slowly, I started to settle into the role and tried my hardest to cover my ears to the chatter flying around. I began going out with friends again, and managed to get back some sort of social life. We'd find trustworthy babysitters or invite friends over to socialise at our house while our daughter – who had stopped crying so much and was sleeping better – slept upstairs. Gradually, I began to feel human again. Our sex life started to resume, especially once I'd learned to masturbate and embraced sex toys. It felt like the fog of early motherhood had lifted – and I was fucking relieved.

Just over two years later, we started talking about having another child. I was firm in my stance that I didn't want to have an only child. I knew what that felt like, having been one myself for 14 years, and it was incredibly lonely. I wanted my daughter to have a team-mate she could always rely on and go to in times of need. But I was shit-scared. I didn't know how I could do it again, but I silenced my fears and I forged ahead anyway because I'm a stubborn fucker. 'Maybe this time it will be different,' I thought. It took a little longer to get pregnant the second time around; about six months, whereas before it happened straight away. I booked a planned C-section because I really didn't want to go through the experience of an emergency one again, and I was incredibly lucky that she was brought into the world in the calmest, most serene way. I've now learned just how much of a privilege it is to have a peaceful birth – and I'm so grateful I got to experience that the second time. Driving to the hospital, knowing we would be having a baby that day, was surreal. I was more prepared this time, more confident and I didn't look for or need the load of other people's opinions. I felt more in charge this time around.

After the birth, my colleagues at the hospital sorted me out with my own room as soon as I was mobile. I restricted visitors and I sent my husband home to be with our oldest daughter. I had the most incredible bonding experience with my newborn baby girl, for the three days I was there. It was just us, quiet and peaceful. I would lay her on my chest, making the most of our skin-to-skin time. She fed when she wanted to, we would nap intermittently throughout the day and I would spend hours looking at her, marvelling at how magical this time was that we had together. It was a complete contrast to my first experience and it was everything I had ever hoped for. This was how I had imagined early motherhood to be, and I finally got to experience the intense beauty of it. She was calmer too; possibly because of her gentle entry into this world, or because I was much more relaxed, or perhaps it was because she had a different temperament to her older sister. If I could, I would go back to that little room we shared in an instant. It makes me emotional thinking back to how special it was.

But, I also felt sad and guilty that I wasn't able to experience that with my first. I know, now, that it's completely normal to not have that instant rainbows-and-butterflies bonding experience with your baby – there are so many factors at play as to why it might not live up to the idealised vision we have in our heads. We have traumatic births, our hormones are all over the place, and some babies are just harder to deal with in the beginning. Looking back, I believe I experienced some degree of postnatal depression, which affects around 1 in 10 women in the UK. For women who suffer, it's a huge challenge and source of shame; we're told that we're built for this job, so when we struggle, it feels like a failure. Regardless of whether you're diagnosed with PND, I think most (if not all) mothers do experience guilt in one way or another, for how they behaved or felt during that introduction to motherhood. I am trying to shed that guilt, because I know that it's not a reflection of who I am as a mother, or my relationship with either of my daughters. If you've ever felt shame about those early days as a new mother – if you found them hard or distressing, or you thought you couldn't do it – please forgive yourself, you were doing your best. I hope you can shed some of that guilt too.

You'd think that motherhood would become more difficult when you have two children rather than one – but I actually found it much smoother. I had a baby and a three-and-a-half-year-old, which probably should've been chaos, but I was more comfortable in the role; I trusted myself, and I knew I was a good mother. Even if I wasn't the zen mum I'd always imagined, I loved my children so much and did my absolute best. My eldest was in nursery school for half the day, most days, so I got some one-on-one time with my baby, and we put a lot of effort into making sure our oldest still felt included and special.

Instead of feeling weighed down by the expectations of motherhood like before, having two girls meant I felt galvanised to strive for a better future for my children. I saw the way they looked to me for guidance, how much they trusted me, and it made me want to do better. They were giving me a strength I didn't know I had, and I pushed myself to be braver for them. I realised that the life of martyrdom and sacrifice we expect from mothers was not one I wanted for my daughters, so why should I want it for myself? It was a revelation – I decided I wanted to start living more authentically and find myself again; I wanted to show them that you don't have to be defined by societal expectations, but by who I knew I could and should be.

First up, I decided I would tackle my body image. I didn't want my girls to grow up hating themselves like I did, and feeling like they didn't belong. One thing I had always wanted to do once in my life was to run a marathon, and, in my youngest daughter's first year, I did just that. Even when I was exhausted from raising two girls, I had more energy and determination this time around, so I would drag myself out of bed, pull on my running shoes and hit the streets. I wanted to train four times a week and push myself harder than I ever had before. It was fucking brutal, and I battled with the guilt of pulling myself away from my family to focus on me. When the day finally arrived, it was extremely tough but incredibly special. My husband and children cheered me on from the sidelines, and when I dragged myself across the finishing line, barely able to walk let alone run, I felt euphoric. I felt immensely proud of what I and my body had achieved, and I'm so glad my daughters were there to witness that. I think everyone could benefit from doing something that hugely challenges them. Something that helps you question everything you previously believed about yourself. Something that allows you to prove to yourself that you're worthy and powerful. For me, it was a marathon. But that's possibly a bit extreme. For you, what might it be?

Running (and walking) for those 26.2 miles switched my mindset about my body on its head, and I learned not to berate myself so much. My body had achieved something incredible, and I decided that it didn't deserve the anger and hatred I channelled into it all the time. I made a resolution to not talk badly about myself any more. Even if I couldn't instantly change my thoughts, I resolved to not let them make their way to my mouth. I decided, once and for all, that I wouldn't ever insult myself verbally. No more looking in the mirror and focusing only on everything I disliked; no more asking, 'do I look big in this?' when trying something on in a clothes-shop changing room. The language we use, the words we say, have a direct impact on how we view ourselves and on how other people view us. Even if we don't feel confident, we can speak kindly to and about ourselves.

Motherhood

The girls had woken me up to how important my position as their caregiver was. I began to challenge and question deeply held beliefs – for them, and for me. We live in an ego-driven, male-centric world that makes women feel like they have to change themselves in the desperate pursuit to belong in a place that wasn't designed for them, knowing that it's futile because we'll never be fully seen, accepted and honoured. I wanted it to be different for my daughters. And even though I felt like I was constantly battling a barrage of negativity and surgery-promoting, fat-phobic rhetoric, I would try to counteract the messages thrown at us from every direction at home.

I knew, without a doubt, that if I was going to challenge society's conditioning and expectations for my children, it had to start with me. I had to dig deep and really look at myself. I had to acknowledge that I was a product of the society I was raised in; I had to own some hard truths. Truths like thinking that my self-worth was strongly linked to my fuckabilty, and the fact that I was exceptionally jealous of other women who I deemed more attractive than me. I said cruel things about women who wore certain clothing that I thought they were too big or too old for, or too pretty to wear. I judged other women harshly who enjoyed sex with multiple people. I was bigoted. I was fearful. I was well-trained to be a misogynistic foot soldier. So many of us are. But it doesn't have to be that way.

Social media helped to open my eyes about how unjust life can be for women. It was revelatory, and I began to talk openly about my journey on Instagram. In my thirties, I was only just beginning to understand that all women have the right to feel valued and beautiful – even if you're not white, thin, attractive (by whatever bullshit beauty standard is currently on-trend) and able-bodied. A huge proportion of women feel like they are invisible and not worthy. I had been one of them.

This shit has to change. We have been fed a very narrow concept of beauty, womanhood and motherhood, making anyone who falls outside of that feel ugly, useless and undeserving. I could see it now. Now I had the ability to see it from a child's perspective – I had a new lens that wasn't clouded by society's rules and expectations. Of course, it still wasn't crystal clear – I am still trying every day to unlearn the concepts I was brought up with. Every single day, I catch myself thinking negative thoughts about myself or others, but what I know is that those thoughts are not me, they have been unsolicitedly given to me. And if I can learn them, I can also unlearn them. My thoughts are not always a true reflection of my untainted soul. The one I was born with. Slowly, I am finding my way back to her again.

Talking to my girls about sex openly, honestly and without embarrassment was another key aspect of my great unlearning. If a child is old enough to ask the question, they are old enough to get a clear, correct answer. Which is why my daughter, aged six, ended up getting that very in-depth description about sex. I think it's extremely important that all parents and guardians try our absolute hardest to raise our children to grow up without the shame we had. My girls know that touching themselves is nothing to be ashamed of. They know that their body parts are theirs, and they can choose to do what they want with them. I have to push past so much awkwardness to convey these messages, but I know I need to lead by example. If mothers can release ourselves from the cage of judgement and shame, we give our children the best possible chance of growing up in freedom.

*

My sex life improved gradually as I regained my confidence, most notably by exploring solo sex more often. It wasn't until I became a mother that I began to understand my body more; what I liked, what felt good and what didn't. I was inching towards sexual empowerment, and I was beginning to be able to make myself climax. I started to get out of my own head and experience pleasure for pleasure's sake.

I found it reassuring when Dr Karen Gurney told me that most people experience lower sexual satisfaction for up to five years after having a baby. It's totally normal. And it's absolutely key to give yourself time, and not pressurise yourself. It's okay for sex to be put on the back-burner for a while, and focus on non-sexual intimacy with your partner (and even friends) instead. That might be simply spending quality time together, or having deep and meaningful conversations. If sex needs to be completely removed from the table, so be it. Your sex drive isn't a use-it-or-lose-it thing – you will get it back. Addressing self-esteem issues, connection with your partner in other ways and carving out time to let yourself be sexy (either alone or with someone else) are all essential pieces of the puzzle.

Although I initially thought that motherhood had ruined my sex life, it ended up improving it more than I ever could've imagined. We have all these ideas that mothers should be on some kind of holy pedestal. There's the notion that women lose all their sex appeal once they have had a child. It's as if the transition into a new stage in life, where you're cleaning up poo and desperately trying to buckle up a car seat, eclipses your ability to desire and be desired. But it's all bullshit, and we need to shift the narrative. Once I pushed past the difficulties of early motherhood, I was able to dig deeper into new, more joyful and pleasurable parts of myself. That's not to say motherhood is the only route to sexual freedom – of course it's not – but that was my experience. I never did find the 'old me', but I think perhaps that was for the best. Instead, I found a version of myself who was bolder, braver, and more open to all that life has to offer.

Repeat after me: 'I can be a sexual, independent, free-thinking being and a good mother all at the same time'. And then say it again until you believe it. These concepts are not mutually exclusive. Yes, having children is a huge deal, and it will change your life in many ways, but most of them are not for the worse. Sure, you can't sleep all day on a hangover any more, and yes, sex has to be more meticulously planned, but my daughters have also helped me become the vibrant, explorative, curious person I am today. A person who no longer feels so shackled by external forces, opinions and expectations. I know that good motherhood isn't about lying down and completely surrendering yourself to the role you've been given. You can still retain your sense of self and even, as in my case, discover an enhanced version of who you truly are. My girls might nick my last sip of water, and they drive me nuts sometimes, but they also give me strength. And strength would beat shame in a fight, any day.

What I've learned about motherhood and sex:

- Motherhood is so glorified and we rarely speak about the realities and difficulties of raising children. Surround yourself with people you can openly share your experiences with. There are so many amazing communities online – if you don't have many mum friends, you could try signing up to Peanut, the social networking app for mums.

- It can take a while to recalibrate your sexual self with your identity as a mother. That's completely okay – allow yourself time. When you feel ready to start exploring sex again, prioritise masturbation and self-exploration. Ease yourself in.

- Remember that everyone's experience with early motherhood is different. For some people, it's a breeze, and, for others, it's extremely hard. Forgive yourself for finding it difficult. It helps to listen to a variety of women's experiences. The podcast 'Happy Mum Happy

Baby' with Giovanna Fletcher is a great example of the expanse of experiences out there.

- Use your kids as motivation to love yourself more, rather than an excuse to love yourself less. Doing things you love, and that fill you with purpose, is the best possible example to set for your kids.

9

Sexuality

'Can I try these on?' she asked, holding an entangled bundle of hangers, dresses and bras.

'Yeah, sure,' I replied.

I was 15 years old, working in a clothes store in Harrow. I loved working there, and they loved me. I was a diligent worker. Even though I was young, the manager was happy to train me up on the till because I had proved I was a trust-worthy member of staff. I thought I was a proper grown-up, working in a proper shop.

This particular morning, I was working in the changing room when she breezed in, giving me a waft of her expen-sive (to my young nostrils, accustomed to smelling Impulse), richly spiced perfume. She got naked in the communal changing room quickly and with ease. She was in a rush, so she asked me to help her. I was putting the clothes back on the hangers as she tried a new item on. It felt like my heart had stopped beating, and my breath was caught in my mouth. I tried not to look at her. I didn't want to make her feel uncomfortable but I could tell that she really didn't care. She was carefree and sophisticated, probably in her late teens, or early twenties. She had dark, shoulder-length hair, brown eyes and the most beautiful body I've ever seen. It was more the air of confidence and lack of inhibitions that really got me though. She seemed comfortable in her own skin, and, having never really felt comfortable in mine, I was enchanted by her.

She left as quickly as she arrived. I searched for her in the shop every day after that, hoping she might breeze in again. She didn't. Looking back, I can't believe I didn't clock on to the fact I was attracted to women. I mean, I had a boyfriend, and I just had an almost-biblical experience with a stranger who rushed in for seven minutes and promptly left again. But I didn't believe I was sexually attracted to her – I just thought I wanted to get to know her; I wanted her to be my best friend. Yet, I can see it more clearly now. I didn't want to be her friend at all – that was certainly not the driving attraction I had to her. Even now, when I think about that moment, it makes me feel warm inside. How can I still remember and conjure up those exact feelings I felt over 25 years ago? The fact this scene is etched into my memory (which isn't great, at the best of times) shows that it made a mark on me. Though, I wouldn't begin to unpack exactly what this moment meant until many years later.

Although Shop Girl was the first woman I remember having a very strong physical reaction to, she wasn't the first girl I'd had a crush on. I would occasionally get obsessed with older girls at school. I would find myself entranced by their hair, or their clothes, or the way they carried themselves, but I never understood this feeling to be anything other than standard female comparison. After all, I had grown up in a culture that pitted girls against each other, that presented women as competing for who could be the 'sexiest' in order to snare a man. The way I felt about them wasn't a crush – no, certainly not. It was a *girl* crush, that classic phrase girls would use to describe other girls they thought were gorgeous and amazing but obviously didn't want to sleep with. It was a completely non-sexual attraction that just *felt* a little bit like attraction. I idolised them; the way they turned boys' heads and seemed to get everything they wanted. They were mesmerising and beautiful, and I knew this because I was so attuned to seeing women through the male gaze. I didn't want to fuck them – I wanted to be them. At least, that's what I had been pre-programmed to believe.

Sometimes, I wonder how different our lives might have been if we had access to today's social media when I was a teenager. If we could've followed amazing queer influencers and celebrities. What would've happened, I wonder, if I'd seen Florence Given's artwork that read: 'maybe it's a girl crush, maybe you're queer.' Would I have questioned those feelings? Would I have dug deeper into what my obsession with girls actually meant? In fact, I wonder whether, if someone had simply asked me if I fancied girls, I would have grappled with the question, and eventually realised the answer was 'yes'? Would you?

At the time, the idea of being sexually attracted to women just wasn't something that felt like an option – especially not for 'good girls'. No, good girls had to do what was expected of them: find a nice boy, marry him, have children. Having a relationship with a girl just didn't seem like a real, legitimate option for me. It's not like I was raised in a homophobic household – if anything, my mum was particularly liberal and she had many gay and trans friends. I remember tagging along to the pub with my mum and a man who my mum had helped dress as a woman for the first time in public. But, of course, there was still a huge stigma surrounding anything outside the heteronormative paradigm when I was a kid, and I know that infiltrated my thoughts. For starters, there was the AIDS pandemic, which led to complete hysteria and fear surrounding homosexual men. But those fears didn't exist in a vacuum – they stemmed from long-lasting, deep-seated cultural worries that sexuality that deviated from the straight, cis norm would somehow harm society.

Gay marriage wasn't legal yet, and gay people's rights continued to lag behind straight people in terms of every-thing from pensions, to eligibility to adopt. Although many people (including my mum) accepted and even celebrated homosexuality, I understood that wider society didn't. I don't remember any of the kids at school coming out as gay, although plenty were teased and called homophobic names, while 'that's so gay' was often used as an insult to mean 'stupid' or 'lame'. I had witnessed my mum's friends, who seemed so open and comfortable in their sexuality, be harassed in public, and I know this affected them. It was clear to me that being gay also meant making your life harder. But more than that, I didn't think to question my own sexuality because heterosexual relationships between men and women were the default.

And, as you know by now, I wanted a life that followed a linear, easy path. I took those expectations of women and I didn't think to question them – in fact, I actively embraced them. I was enamoured by the heteronormative relationships I saw in my favourite movies – *Dirty Dancing*, *Pretty Woman*, *Karate Kid*, *Flashdance* – and literature like *Jane Eyre* – the first 'proper' book I remember reading. Men existed to save women. Women existed to serve men. The relationships seemed mutual and rewarding, both parties balancing the other out. I wanted a happy ending. My mind was completely boxed off from the possibility that loving a woman could fit into that. I admired people who chose to live authentically and freely, loving who they wanted to love, and I saw myself as an ally to the LGBTQ+ community. But I just genuinely didn't believe I was one of those people. How could I be gay, when I was boy-hungry? I had been well-trained to view myself through the male gaze. Men occupied my thoughts at all times. I had a couple of boyfriends and then met my now ex-husband, and everything seemed to be as it should. I revelled in male attention. I wanted, desperately, to be wanted by men. And wasn't that the most important thing?

Yet, my attraction to women remained a lingering sensation in my life. I've snogged women on nights out for as long as I can remember; stealing drunken kisses (usually initiated by me, when alcohol would lower my inhibitions) in bathroom stalls with friends, or random women I'd shared lipstick with. Kissing has always been my thing, and I'd tell myself that snogging women was nothing sexual – that it was just something fun; a bonding experience. I didn't keep it a secret from my partner – he knew about it and, while I don't think he relished the idea, he was fairly accepting that it was just something I did occasionally, and it didn't mean anything too deep.

While these kisses were always stolen in private, I did know girls who would kiss other women in front of their boyfriends (or any male bystanders), simply because they knew it looked sexy. It's undeniable that girl-on-girl action is sexualised and fetishised – you only have to see how big and popular the lesbian sections on porn sites are – and I think part of this comes down to the sexualisation of women's bodies more broadly. So when you have two hyper-sexualised people put together, what do you get? A load of men with massive hard-ons. But this idea is pretty problematic too, because it also undermines the lesbian experience as one built on love, respect and emotions. It makes many people believe that lesbians exist to satisfy the male gaze, stripping away their autonomy. In fact, one fucked-up study by a Cypriot professor from 2017 claimed that lesbian relationships only exist because men find it a turn-on. I mean, really?

This also partly explains why the stigma surrounding male homosexuality and female homosexuality differs so much – with gay men getting a really raw deal. Gay sex was only decriminalised between two consenting adults in 1967, but this only applied to men. There was no such law criminalising it between two women. Why? According to some historians, Queen Victoria insisted that proper 'ladies' would never do such things. Others suggest that it was because lesbian sex was deemed impossible – probably because penetration was considered to be the only form of legitimate sex. I imagine, too, that women being intimate with other women didn't cause the same moral outrage as men having sex with men, because of patriarchal expect-ations that men should retain power and dominance over women. That they shouldn't be effeminate, because, after all, femininity was the lowest of the low. All of this meant that, while homosexuality as a whole was given the stamp of moral badness, lesbianism also had a sexy yet frivolous vibe. The message was: women wouldn't do that, but if they're going to, they better make sure it's appealing and palatable for men's lustful eyes.

Despite convincing myself that the kissing was just a 'thing' I did, and not linked to any deeper sexual desire, I fantasised about women. A lot of the time I'd fantasise about threesomes – often with two women and one man, and sometimes it was just women. Again I rationalised this as being down to lesbian porn I had watched. Women's bodies, I'd say, are just far sexier than men's – hence the obsession surrounding them. I mean, who wouldn't be turned on by gorgeous, soft curves and full breasts? I still strongly believe you can have fantasies that don't necessar-ily match up to what you'd want to do in real life, but, sometimes, this can be an excuse we tell ourselves in order to suppress our deepest desires. 'So what, I imagine having sex with women – that doesn't make me a lesbian!' I'd protest, to my own brain. I think so many of us ignore our

Feeling Myself

deepest desires, because it's simply too scary to imagine the alternative. To veer off-path, to completely edit the storyline of a script we've spent our whole lives writing. Before we can even get to admitting those desires to other people, the hardest part is admitting them to ourselves.

Throughout my twenties, within the safety of my own brain, I'd occasionally daydream about myself in a relationship with a woman. Not just sex, but an actual relationship. I knew that porn was an unrealistic depiction of lesbian sex, and I wanted to know how women came together when no one else was watching. I wondered what it would feel like; what it would taste like. I wanted to experience that closeness, both physically and emotionally.

At first, I tried to push these thoughts away. But as I started to become more liberated in other parts of my life, exploring sex positivity online, and embracing self-pleasure, I began to tune into them. For the first time, I decided to listen to my desires, without giving them excuses. I wanted to know whether my attraction to women was simply an intoxicated thrill or if it was something deeper. In many ways, I was scared. I was in a relationship, married with two kids. If I did have an emotional and sexual connection with a woman, would my whole world fall apart? Or would it confirm that drunken kisses were the furthest it would ever go?

*

The first time I had an emotional and sexual connection with a woman, it was completely different to anything I'd

200

experienced before. I met her at a mutual friend's party, after the dust had settled on my separation. The friend introduced us because she thought we'd get along, and she was right. I was instantly attracted to her – she had a cute pixie cut and a confident demeanour that made me want to get to know her better. I knew that she was gay, and I could tell that she was flirting with me. After spending the whole night chatting, we met up again for a drink. I was intrigued, I wasn't completely sure if I liked her or not. Roll on two hours and it was clear that we both liked each other *a lot*. I'm not sure how we got from A to B, but we ended up in the bathroom of the bar, kissing passionately, with our hands roaming everywhere. But this time, it was different. This time, it wasn't just a drunken kiss. I really fancied her, and I wanted it to go further. And thankfully, she did too. I was so overwhelmed with desire (and probably a little drunk) that I didn't even feel nervous when she slid her hand into my jeans. I'd imagined that it would be some huge moment for me, but actually it felt so natural and right. We ended up doing all kinds of things in that bathroom that I probably shouldn't repeat here. But all I can say is we both ended up climaxing on the cubicle floor while revellers banged on the door. Definitely the hottest sex I've ever had.

We carried on seeing each other for a couple of months. When we were together, the chemistry was electric. But much more important than your bits getting tingly was the feeling of being home. Let's call it 'a connected knowing'. It never felt forced or unnatural. When things moved away from the toilet floor, I did sometimes struggle to orgasm in the times that followed, and it would take me a while to let myself really go and relax (when I wasn't drunk). I still felt very strange about the newness of the relationship, having spent so long with one man. But that didn't take anything away from the excitement, the connection and the cosy feeling that I had when we snuggled up in bed together. Being touched by a woman who knows what it feels like to be touched the way a woman likes to be touched is nothing short of sensational. I really hoped this wasn't a fluke and I had just lucked out.

Once I was able to relax and get out of my head, the sex hit at a new, different level. The beauty of it was that it didn't feel routine. It was different every time; sometimes we'd use toys, sometimes just our fingers and tongues. It flowed easily and naturally and seemed to be guided by feeling, rather than a formulaic structure like when I had sex with a man. We experimented all the time, with techniques, positions, different toys and even breath play. We checked in constantly, watching closely for each other's reactions and verbally by asking. There seemed to be much more focus on the subtleties involved in two bodies coming together. Much more communication and a hell of a lot more consideration of each other's wants and needs. Things like dressing up seemed to be obsolete, at least in our partnership – that felt tacky and male-gaze driven. I didn't feel the pressure to shave or worry about how I looked so much. I felt less judged for my scars, wobbles, cellulite and body size. That's not to say my male partners ever made me feel criticised or unwanted because of my body – they didn't. But there was just a new kind of carefreeness with a woman. Less performing. Less expectation. More under-standing. Greater freedom.

Falling for a woman was powerful and painful. It felt like the warm, delicious sensation of being home while the wind, rain and hailstones crashed and tumbled down from the sky outside. We would alternate between being comfort-ably wrapped up in one another, to hot, sweaty skin-on-skin rawness. It felt safe and familiar yet strange and exciting. Was this what I'd been waiting for my whole life? Suddenly I wasn't lining up in a queue any more, hoping my life was about to start. I had always had this feeling that there was more for me out there; I was never fully satisfied but I couldn't put my finger on why. I had done all the things I was supposed to do to make me fulfilled – I had the Victorian terraced house, the car, the husband, the two kids, and a house full of pets. I had always wondered why that wasn't enough. Suddenly everything made sense – I had been ignoring a part of myself for so long.

When I spoke to Zayna Ratty, an intersectional psycho-therapist who specialises in diverse relationships, she told me that embracing your true identity is essential to having a strong sense of self.

'Not being authentic to the intersectionality of your identity won't do you any favours in the long term,' she said. 'Dissociation isn't your friend. A centred self isn't to be confused with being self-centred. Thinking about your sexuality won't make you less of yourself, only more of yourself.'

When we allow ourselves to be really, deeply, true to who we are – which includes our sexuality and desires – I believe this is where we can find that sense of contentment we're all looking for. If we are willing to scratch out our pre-destined scripts with a big, chaotic scribble in thick black marker ink, we can actually find that the story is more rewarding, and more beautiful, than anything we could've imagined. It took me almost four decades to learn that.

Our love affair was complicated, because women (and of course I'm generalising here, but this is my experience) think very deeply; everything is analysed and challenged. A wrong look or snide remark – nothing goes unnoticed. Being in a relationship is like a mirror, in some ways it exacerbated my worst traits and made me very aware of my role in the relationship and in conflicts. The collisions were explosive and painful and when the attraction to the adren-aline rush of the highs and lows wavers, the work begins. Or doesn't. That's when I decided to walk away because I knew I needed a more stable, adult, healthy relationship. Still, falling in love with her taught me so much – about myself, about other women, about everything. I'll always be grateful that it happened.

Now, I would describe myself as pansexual, which means I'm attracted to souls rather than genitalia – but I guess 'bisexual' works too. I struggle with labels; they can be amazing, because they can connect us with like-minded people. But they can also feel restrictive, as they come with expectations and, again, assumptions. As a bisexual woman who has spent most of her life in a relationship with cis men (and possibly will again), I used to feel like a fraud and certainly not part of the LGBTQ+ community. I think it was largely because I was in the final years of my marriage and

Sexuality

I desperately wanted to be included, but I wasn't out and open yet. I was in a heterosexual relationship and I didn't know how to express my sexuality without feeling like I was upsetting or betraying my partner. I now realise that embracing your sexuality doesn't negate or undermine a relationship if you're with someone of the opposite sex. For some reason, we've decided that, unless you're in a non-heterosexual relationship, you can't possibly be queer. But it's ridiculous: being pan or bi means that you can fall in love with people from multiple sexes and gender identities, and your identity is valid, no matter who you're currently in love with. And I've since realised that the queer community is a vibrant and welcoming space, and you can belong there just as much as you belong anywhere else in the world.

That said, unpacking my sexuality has been a complicated and tricky experience. I started to wonder whether perhaps I was only attracted to men for the stability aspect. I noticed that I was definitely more attracted to ambitious, financially secure men. I liked the feeling of being cared for. Could this be down to social conditioning? Quite possibly. Girls are socialised from day dot to believe that we need the care and affection of a man in order to be able to function as a woman. I saw men as being my saviour, my protector. Was this just a self-esteem issue on my part? I'm not sure. Despite the fact I still fantasise about men and watch straight porn, I think I am more attracted to women physically, and emotionally. The power dynamic when you're with another woman is refreshing and equal – there's something wonderful about having a partner who is fighting the same battles against body issues and social conditioning. There's a deeper understanding that just isn't there with a man. Like having an incredible friend, except with more sex, it can feel spiritual and magical to connect with a woman. Now, I'm not saying you should divorce your husband and run off into the sunset with a woman ;) but I'd love you to question the deeply held beliefs about who you are, why you're attracted to the people you're attracted to, and what kind of life would make you feel most like your true self. Is your sexuality built on social expectations? Or is it reflective of your innermost desires?

I believe that sexuality is fluid, ever-changing and evolving. In fact, scientists have been saying this since the 1940s (but I'm not sure very many of us were listening). In 1948, American doctors Alfred Kinsey, Wardell Pomeroy and Clyde Martin developed the Heterosexual–Homosexual Rating Scale – otherwise known as the Kinsey Scale – after studying people's sexual histories and preferences. Their findings showed that people did not fit into exclusive heterosexual and homosexual categories, and that their sexual behaviour, thoughts and feelings shifted over time.

Intersectional psychotherapist Zayna Ratty agrees with this theory. 'Suggesting sexuality isn't a spectrum is a binaried way of looking at the scope of expression of affection, that can be sexual, intimate, romantic or emotional,' she told me. 'Fixed – and possibly artificial – categories can be a gateway to understanding yet can keep us in boxes and within labels that we may feel unable to break free from.'

Of course, for many people, their sexualities might feel defined and solid, but that isn't the experience for everyone. And personally, I think that's reassuring for anyone who is questioning or unsure. You don't need to feel or identify as one thing. You can allow yourself to follow your desires. They can change throughout your life, and they can change in a given moment.

I never had the feeling of wanting to 'come out' – I've had a slow unravelling process about my attraction to both sexes, that mostly began after my marriage ended. I'm very open about it. But that's pretty much an extension of who I have become over the past few years – I'm sure you know by now that I don't shy away from rawness and honesty. But it's also about luck. I'm really lucky to have supportive family and friends who don't judge me, or think it's a big deal in any way. In fact, many of my loved ones understand that sexuality is a spectrum too, so they were hardly surprised. But I know this isn't everyone's experience. Being open about your sexuality can be a really frightening experience, and can feel like a huge mountain to climb.

If you're scared about the idea of 'coming out' to loved ones, Zayna Ratty advises that you go gently. 'Come out to yourself first and practise self-compassion,' she said. 'This isn't easy for anyone to do, as in many cultures and societies, heterosexuality is the sociocultural default.' You might want to practise doing it in front of the mirror, planning exactly what you want to say and how you want to say it. Only you can know when you're ready to show this part of your authentic self to other people. Choose your timing and don't let anyone pressure you to do something sooner or later to what feels right for you.

'Internalised conditioned phobia and shame affects many in the community, so go easy on yourself,' suggested

Zayna. 'Search out where to find help and assistance, whether that's a trusted friend, chosen family or professional.' And whatever the outcome of that conversation, Zayna said, 'never forget you are worthy of being valued and respected.' Even if it's too hard to tell your elderly religious grandma, or your judgemental brother, about your sexuality, the most important thing is that you're honest with yourself.

My hope is that, one day, coming out won't be a necessity – for *anyone*. As soon as children are born, we assume they are straight. Even when they're in primary school, we ask boys if they have girlfriends, and we ask girls if they have boyfriends. Why? How could we possibly know where their attraction lies, and who they could end up loving? These assumptions – this idea that heterosexuality is the default – is so damaging, and I know for sure that it explains why I didn't think I could ever have a relationship with a woman. I was just straight, automatically, and I had to go out of my way to explore the possibility that this wasn't necessarily the path for me. I imagine there are a whole generation of people who are trapped inside relationships and marriages with the opposite sex, because they just didn't know there was any other way.

I like to think things are starting to change – LGBTQ+ family set-ups are finally being taught on the curriculum, helping children to understand that there are a variety of different, valid and loving, family structures and relationships. There is more queer representation on TV and in movies – from *Feel Good* to *Euphoria* to *Call Me by Your Name* to *Single All the Way* – and I don't think we can underestimate the power of normalising beautiful, diverse relationships. The rainbow flag is instantly recognisable. 'Love is love' is less a cheesy Instagram quote and more a global battle cry. The way we are defining what is the 'default' is shifting. Thank fuck for that.

I try not to assume my girls are straight – we talk openly about having crushes on celebrities of multiple genders, and I would never assume they are going to end up with a man, or anyone else. I wonder if I had been brought up and taught this way, whether it would have taken me until my thirties to explore my attraction to women. I guess we'll never know. But at least we can all try to avoid making the same mistakes with our children. If you define yourself as heterosexual, you can be a real ally to the LGBTQ+ community by normalising queer love, and teaching your children that there isn't one default of sexuality. We all have a role to play in shifting our future consciousness.

Though, it's still hard to live in this world authentically and freely. The vast majority of the planet is stuck in a homophobic frame of mind, enforcing strict rules about who is allowed to love and desire who. Even after going on the journey that I have, I still have to force myself to unpack internalised homophobia, misogyny, and question my own judgements and assumptions every day. I'm not sure how humankind got into this mess, where we think we have so much control over our own sexual urges and emotions, and we have the right to police other people's. But slowly, with more awareness, we can unlearn all the damage we have done.

Who knows how I'll feel next year, or even next week, and I have no idea who I'll have sex with, or fall in love with, next. But I think that's the beauty of sexuality. It's not a fixed, binary, permanent state of being. And that is so exciting! There are likely people I haven't met who will become a profound part of my sexual and love life, and I have no idea who they are yet. The uncertainty of life is what makes it so fulfilling, and embracing the messiness of your sexuality can crack your world wide open. We no longer need to be confined by the traditional lives and expectations laid out for us. You don't have to feel ashamed for your normal, natural desires, that might just involve your same sex or gender. There's so much more potential for sexual experience and intimacy, if only you are willing to expand your mind and give yourself permission to go for it. You can be anyone you want to be, and love anyone you want to love. That, really, is sexual freedom.

What I've learned about sexuality:

- It's okay to not really know where you sit on the sexuality spectrum. Don't rush to put a label on yourself. It's okay to be curious, and look for ways to explore your sexuality that are consensual and safe. You don't need to put yourself in a box.

- Take the time to learn about the LGBTQ+ community, and speak up on important causes. There are some great Instagram accounts you can learn from – I love Matt Bernstein (@mattxiv) and Char Ellesse

Sexuality

(@ellessechar) – but it's important to do your own research too, outside of social media.

- If you're only starting to explore your sexuality, have clear communication with anyone you date so they don't feel you're only using them as an experiment. Be upfront about any nervousness, and be clear about what you're looking for.

- Openly embracing your sexuality is just one way of embracing who you truly are. There are so many others: maybe it's about the way you dress, or the interests you've always felt ashamed of admitting. How can you learn to live as your true, authentic self?

10

Sex After Separation

Deciding to end my marriage was the hardest decision of my life. There were many times where I nearly did it, but I backtracked, because I felt like we should give it another go. Maybe we just needed to go to more therapy, make more effort, have more sex. Although I was unhappy, I'd reflect back on what we'd been through, what we'd built together and how much love was there. Even though we couldn't talk about the hard stuff without a therapist in the room, I'd decide that our relationship was worth saving. I'd give myself some arbitrary deadline – 'if it's not better by then, I'll do it,' I'd tell myself more times than I can remember. But that date would come around, and nothing had really improved, but there was always something else that stopped me in my tracks. It couldn't possibly happen near one of the kids' birthdays, and I didn't want the girls to forever associate Christmas with the time their parents split up. There never seemed to be a perfect time.

Eventually, the end was uneventful. It was early June 2020, the month of both of our 40th birthdays, and in the height of lockdown. It turns out that breaking up during a global pandemic was pretty unoriginal – charity Citizens Advice reported a spike in online searches about ending relationships during the first lockdown. The intensity of being stuck inside during the pandemic definitely wasn't the reason we broke up, but I think it was probably the trigger I needed. It brought everything up to the surface, making it too hard to ignore the discomfort and pretend everything was okay. We were both in the bedroom getting dressed. I can't remember what precipitated it – whether we were arguing, or doing our own thing. There was an awkward silence – I sat down on the bed and hung my head low. 'I can't do this any more,' I said, shaking. I was sad, and scared about how he'd react, but also completely resigned to the fact we had tried everything. I had nothing left in me.

He instantly knew what I was talking about. We had just been surviving for such a long time. We didn't enjoy each other's company; our communication and intimacy had been lost a long time ago. I was doing anything and everything I could not to be around – the feeling of being trapped, isolated and suffocated was only exacerbated during the pandemic. I would escape to parks, supermarkets, and see friends outside whenever I could. He was getting angry that I wasn't around. When he was at home, I wasn't. When he was at work, I was at home. When we were in the same room together, it was too painful; the air was thick with unspoken feelings. Even though therapy had led to a greater sense of understanding, there was still too much we couldn't fix.

Yet, I still didn't hate him. I loved him. I think that's why it felt even harder. He had been there throughout so much of my life; a sturdy pillar I had always relied on. He was – is – a good man. He worked hard. He looked after his family, including me, so well. But there was just something missing. When there's no big reason for separating, it makes the decision agonising. I would question myself, not trusting my own feelings and having constant arguments with my own brain. Why can't you just make this work? Why can't it be like how it used to be? Even: why are you making a problem out of nothing? It sounds terrible, but sometimes I thought I would've preferred him to be a cunt – abusive or controlling or cheating – because at least then I'd have a 'valid' reason for wanting to leave. I'm sure some of this comes down to childhood issues of seeing so many awful men. Feeling like I'd hit the jackpot and not understanding why I wasn't happy – he was a good man. I think, a lot of the time, women don't trust our own instincts. We think we should feel lucky to have the love of a good, kind-hearted man. So, we ignore our feelings of discontent, dismissing our desire for greater joy as greedy. I guess we're raised to believe that we don't deserve a place in this world, so it's not surprising that so many of us have an ingrained belief that we don't deserve to be happy.

Eventually, I reasoned with myself that he would be happier without me; that he deserved to be with someone who desperately wanted him too. I convinced myself that my happiness *was* important – that even though ending a marriage would be devastating for our kids, seeing their parents finding happiness would make them happier, too. Right? I told myself this, repeatedly, and yet still I was unconvinced. I felt incredibly guilty. All I wanted was for my kids to have a stable two-parent home – the home I'd craved as a child. I know how messed up I was from my dad's absence and, although I know their father is nothing like mine, I couldn't help beating myself up for snatching their idyllic, secure childhood away from them. Even now, as I write this more than a year on, the guilt still sucker-punches me in the solar plexus now and again. It probably always will.

I thought I was doing one of the worst things a parent can do by ending my relationship, but of course, divorce is incredibly common and more children now grow up in single-parent households than ever before. Estimates suggest a whopping 42% of marriages in England and Wales end in divorce. The number just keeps increasing, and I think it's because so many of us are no longer willing to settle for staying in relationships that are making us unhappy. There has been a culture shift in recent years: we shouldn't have to suffer, and 'stay for the kids' at the detriment of our own happiness and health. Ultimately, that's a great thing. I decided that having role models who are happy was a much better option for my children. When the shame and guilt threatens to take over, I try to remember that. Kids are remarkably resilient. And we all deserve to be happy.

I'm well-versed in disassociating from my feelings when everything feels overwhelming, and the separation was a prime example. I couldn't articulate my emotions because I didn't even know how I was feeling. The heavy burden of indecision had lifted, which made me feel lighter – but other than that, I couldn't name or connect with how I felt. I just got on with the day-to-day necessities of surviving and manoeuvring through the change, taking each step as it came. We still had to live together and share the same bed for a few months because of practicalities and Covid. It felt weirdly normal, seeing as we were used to not talking about what was really going on and keeping things surface-level and polite. We were like two planets in orbit around the kids – crossing paths, but mostly in our own worlds.

I wish I had confided in more friends during that time. They didn't have any idea what was happening until very near the end. I went into shut-down mode, and I expected everyone to blame me for not being able to make it work. I had resigned myself to the fact that our shared friends would choose him – and I was fine with that if it meant I didn't have to answer intrusive questions. He has always been much more personable and sociable than me; he's a showman and everyone who meets him loves him. I presumed he'd communicate his problems much better than I ever could. But I do my friends a disservice; there are some who do really get me. They don't need me to explain and will just be there, and for them I am forever grateful. I'm so good at delving deep into other people's issues, looking after them and knowing exactly what it is that they need when big life-changing events happen to them. But, when it's me, I don't know how to be open and vulnerable with those closest to me.

Being single has taught me that we all need to move past that idea. I think there's a tendency for women especially to think we have to appear to have everything under control. That admitting we need help and support is representative of some kind of deeper failure. I gradually started to learn that accepting help is nothing to be ashamed of. One of my friends had been through divorce before and she was really helpful in advising me on the divorce process and the feelings it would bring up. She's also much more financially savvy than me and advised on how it would work financially and fairly. Utilising your friends' talents and expertise can be really valuable.

I was so enveloped in thinking about the present situation, navigating the strange period of transition, that I had given no time to thinking about the future. I didn't consider what it would be like to co-parent, and that I'd often be alone when the kids were with their dad. I didn't think about the fact that I'd be single. That at some point, I might start dating. I'm not sure I allowed myself to think about it because the thought was too scary. I hadn't been alone since I was 16 years old. I simply didn't know what being on my own felt like. Even in the most practical sense, it was terrifying. When my ex eventually moved out and the kids stayed with him the first few times, I felt so lonely and afraid. I couldn't sleep. What if someone burgled the house, ransacking the downstairs while I was here in bed? I had no man to nudge awake and send downstairs with a baseball bat in hand any more. It was just me, and I felt exposed and unsafe. I heard every creak and imagined footsteps creeping up the stairs. When the kids were at home with just me, the fear was there too. What if someone attacked us and I couldn't protect my girls, like their dad would? My thoughts would spiral as I'd catastrophise all the ways my decision to separate might somehow hurt the people I loved most.

The day-to-day of domestic life was full of reminders about how different my life was going to be. I'd remember that no one else is going to empty the bin, no matter how long I leave it or how badly it smells. And the jungle in the back garden ain't going to be magically eaten by a herd of cows. When I noticed that my daughter's door hadn't had a door knob on it for six months and she had to precariously open it with a pen stuck in the hole, I knew it was about time to buy myself some tools and just get on with it myself. That was a learning curve, let me tell you.

The sense of achievement I felt the first time I mowed the lawn, an area always reserved for my husband, was immense. I didn't know I could do it on my own. I know it sounds ridiculous – of course I could do it. But I'd just never done it. No matter how emancipated and independent I thought I was, I realised I had been harbouring a lot of internalised stereotypes and sexism about men and women's roles in the home. Without realising it, we had fallen into the traditional traps – I had taken on the lion's share of the cooking and housework, while he dealt with the bills, bins, garden and car. But the separation uncovered so many skills that I would have never associated with myself. The first time I got out my electric drill and put up a blind in one of the kids' bedrooms, I felt like a motherfucking tooled-up superhero.

It's moments like these that make me feel grateful for this new period of being on my own. For years, I felt stupid and silly, and doubted my abilities. Women are so often led to believe that certain things aren't 'for' them – anything that involves a little engineering, a little maths. It's the reason why so many careers are still overwhelmingly male-dominated. But it's bullshit. Who says men are better at DIY? Who says women are better at cleaning toilets? Just because these ideas are the norm doesn't mean we have to listen to them. If you're in a relationship, I hope you question these roles – is it actually true that you can't handle the bills? Or have you just been infantilised because you're female? I've learned so fucking much in such a short space of time, and I'm trying to celebrate those wins – and ensure all women know they're capable of doing what needs to be done. I don't know you personally, but I can almost guarantee that you aren't as stupid or silly as you think you are.

But being single, after a lifetime of long-term relationships, has also been confronting. Once he had moved out, friends convinced me that I should get on the dating apps. I had never dated in the real world before, let alone online, so the thought of it was terrifying – but I was also curious. It was a whole new world for me. But flicking through pictures of people, reading their carefully constructed answers to pointless questions, made me feel sad. I had one particular app downloaded for a whole 24 hours, before freaking out and deleting it. It all felt so alien to me, and the idea of meeting people in person seemed like a lot of effort. To start afresh with someone, to have someone else learn all my flaws and struggles, and for me to learn all of theirs? I'd become exhausted just thinking about it. The idea of telling my story over and over again on dates, that probably wouldn't go anywhere, didn't excite me in the slightest.

And if talking felt scary, the idea of sex felt fucking petrifying. To strip back all my layers, to reveal such a vulnerable side of myself, was not something I felt ready for at all. I'd worked so hard to build up my confidence and assertiveness in my own sexuality, and I was conscious that someone – especially a man – could trample on that all over again. I decided that I was still too sensitive, too analytical, too damaged, to engage in mindless sex and not feel empty and deflated afterwards. I was careful to protect myself and not do anything that was risky as I was very emotionally fragile. Jumping into bed with a stranger was the last thing on my mind.

*

I had always dreamed of having a relationship with a woman and I did; in fact, I've had multiple. It was an odd time and I was still processing my marriage and where it went wrong. I'm thankful, though, that the first person I had sex with after the end of my marriage was someone I had an incredible connection with. She was the first woman I had allowed myself to be both physically and emotionally vulnerable with, and I loved being around her. Despite this, I struggled to relax and be in the moment. Something was holding me back. Whether it was guilt for my marriage ending, my self-esteem issues or just not knowing whether I could completely trust her, or a combination of all three – I don't know. But I often struggled to orgasm. It would take a long time. I would get frustrated and I felt bad that she was trying so hard and I wasn't reaching, even though I seriously fancied her, which made me get lost in my head even more. Giving felt much easier than receiving; making her come came naturally. I got a lot of pleasure out of seeing how easily and beautifully she was able to have multiple orgasms one after another.

But she was so generous, understanding and patient with me, and eventually I would learn how to relax, lie back and receive pleasure myself, but it took time to get there. When you've been in a relationship for so long, having the same kind of sex for such a long time, it can be a peculiar sensation to adjust to a new person, with all their own sexual quirks, likes and dislikes. Letting my guard down, and communicating openly with her, helped. Forgiving myself for finding the transition weird helped too. It won't necessarily feel normal straight away, and that's more than okay.

It was reassuring to know that I wasn't alone in struggling with erotic intimacy after separation. When I spoke to Rosie Green, the hilarious magazine columnist and author of *How to Heal a Broken Heart*, she had a similar experience. Like me, Rosie had been with her husband since her teens, so singledom was uncharted territory.

'Having been with my husband for 26 years, we'd developed this sort of sexual script, and essentially we'd been having the same kind of sex for that whole time,' she said. 'When we first got together, I was still nervous, shy and sexually inexperienced. I was still trying to be a "good girl" and had a lot of shame and guilt surrounding sex, so I think that carried on throughout my relationship.'

Feeling Myself

After dealing with the fallout of her heartbreak, Rosie was ready – but scared – to get back in the saddle. 'I wanted that closeness and intimacy. I wanted to feel desired again,' she recalled. 'But naturally I was anxious about sex because I'd never entered into a sexual relationship as a grown-up. The idea that I could go out on three dates and then sleep with someone. I thought: can I do that? Is that allowed? Will the morality police come and shoot me? I had equated sex with love at all times.'

But, like me, Rosie eventually found that sex, free from the confines of a long-term relationship, could be magical. 'Suddenly thinking about sex in terms of being in the moment, the pleasure, the endorphins . . . it was a revelation,' she said. Becoming single after a decades-long relationship can be a unique time to learn that sex doesn't need to be something you 'have' to do in order to maintain marital harmony. It can be about you: your desire, your pleasure, your exploration. I think this is a monumental lesson to learn, but you don't have to be single to understand this. Even if you are in a relationship, you can integrate these lessons into how you have sex, right now.

My good friend Helen Thorn, aka one half of The Scummy Mummies and author of *Get Divorced, Be Happy*, experienced a similar realisation: 'One of the things I was most surprised about,' she told me, 'was how the moment he left, my libido came flooding back like a tsunami. I couldn't stop wanking and wanted to be fucked really hard. That was exciting, confusing and confronting. I had gone from being prudish, not wanking very much, hardly owning a sex toy, to the exact opposite.'

Clearly, knowing you deserve to enjoy yourself is a big part of embracing sex after separation. I know I had always found that the intensity of having sex with someone you love (or just like a lot) is pretty special; the security and comfort of that can be key ingredients for the vulnerability and surrender that good sex requires. But casual shags can sometimes allow for more surrender, in their own way – because there's a certain freedom to them. There's less expectation and you won't have built-up feelings like resentment that can block your orgasms.

For Helen, this was definitely the case. 'I was on one of the dating apps and I matched with this really young, hot guy,' she told me. 'We matched at 6pm, met at 9pm and by 11pm we were fucking in my house. He was confident, he liked older women and he was there for my pleasure. He wanted me to have orgasms, and at the end of the sex, we were comparing people we'd matched on the apps, and we spoke openly about pleasure and desire. Then, at 2am, he left. It was frank, open, consensual, and a really fucking hot experience.'

Brief encounters clearly work for Helen, but I've always found them to be fraught with difficult feelings. I'd struggle to let go and be present with a new person, and my self-esteem issues would creep in and make me feel icky about the whole thing. Because of this, the beginnings of my single life felt especially daunting. I think I have always been a relationship person, and I still find it hard to push past the barriers of vulnerability to open myself up to total strangers. 'But my brilliant friend Cherry Healey is pretty convincing about why, for some, they can be a positive, healthy experience.

'Sex is as deep as the ocean and yet we splish-splash about on the shore and never fucking get our wetsuit on and get in,' she told me. 'When my relationship ended, I had to give myself a slap around the face and ask myself: "Do I want to live a life where I'm missing out on this wonderful ocean?" I didn't want to get to 85 years old and regret that I never got in the sea. I looked at it, sat by it, and never got in. And part of learning about sex is not feeling shame around it. After I ended my relationship I had two one-night stands and actively chose not to feel any shame – why would I? Because society has told women that men can do it but for women it is "sinful"?!

'As long as you always make sure you're safe, they can be really exciting,' Cherry said. 'It's such a thrill – it's like going skinny-dipping. I have quite a routined life; I have two kids. I turn up at work on time. So sometimes it's fun to just take off all your clothes and jump into the sea.'

I love Cherry's approach – even if it is something I'm still getting to grips with. Perhaps we should view casual sex as just one other way of pushing yourself out of your comfort zone, and that's something I'm constantly trying to do more of

That said, I also think it's important to follow your instincts, and never do anything you're not comfortable with. Some people need spontaneity and adventure to feel the most pleasure, while others need 500 conversations plus a few sessions of heavy-petting before they can let loose enough to have an orgasm with someone. When you're newly single, there can be a lot of pressure to 'get out there' and do all the shagging you had been missing out on, but we all go at different paces, and want different things. Leave your comfort zone if you want to, but if you want to stay firmly inside its bounds, there's no shame in that either.

It's also important to remember that the casual sex and dating world can be rough. I know I'm not the only one who has found the dating apps terrifying – and Helen recommends treading with caution. 'Don't rush into online dating right away,' she advised. 'It can be really brutal, and if you're feeling vulnerable, it can escalate that. Sex is so easy to get. In London, you can get it in about three hours. It can literally fill a hole. But if you confuse sex with love, that's an issue too.'

So how can you prep yourself for the big bad world of online (or real-life) dating? 'Start with self-love,' Helen suggested. 'Learn what turns you on, learn what makes you feel sexy. Someone told me: buy a whole load of new lingerie. Treat yourself, have a date night with yourself first, run a bath, play music and feel the sexual energy when you're alone.'

Rosie agreed: 'Spend a little time finding your confidence again. Even if you don't believe it, write down what you like about yourself. Make sure you have a good measure of your self-worth.' I think you should also spend a lot of time wanking. Being self-sufficient in your own pleasure, enjoying your own body and knowing what does and doesn't turn you on, will help you feel much more comfortable when you do eventually decide to open yourself up (literally and metaphorically) to someone else.

When you do feel ready to get on the apps, Cherry has these golden rules: 'Write your profile with integrity. If you have kids, say you have kids. If you have something you find difficult to talk about, write it in your profile, so you avoid time-wasters. Always meet equal distance between you. Don't get dating fatigue. If you are starting to get a bit bored, take a break.'

But it's not just the nerves about vulnerability that can cause dating-fear – there's, of course, the very real fear of safety. This is something I have struggled with, especially when it comes to men. I think that's why it felt so much easier to have my first post-marriage relationships with women.

Cherry had some great advice for navigating one-night stands. 'Always make sure your phone is fully charged,' she said. 'If your phone is out of battery, you never go anywhere with someone. And make sure your friends know exactly who you are with and where you are. Finally and most importantly, at every point on a date, remember to check in with yourself. Ask: Am I too drunk? If you are, go home. Ask yourself if you're having a lovely time. Ask yourself if there are any red flags.'

'Trust your gut instinct,' Helen agreed. 'I always try to have a phone conversation with the person beforehand. When I've ignored that rule, it hasn't gone well. Create boundaries and say beforehand what you like and don't like.'

As I tentatively step into my own new chapter of single life, speaking to Helen, Rosie and Cherry reassures me so much about what I have ahead of me. They all told me they feel more sexually empowered than ever. Isn't that fucking amazing? That women who don't have a long-term relationship with a man to define them, can actually feel like their best selves? But I know it's not just about separating – I'm pretty sure a lot of it comes with the territory of getting older and wiser. I think that dating when you're not worrying so much about what everyone else thinks of you will always be a much more invigorating and joyful experience. You're much more self-assured; you accept your flaws and you know what you want, and what you need.

'My thinking as a woman dating in her mid-thirties is: "you're very lucky if you get to be with me",' Cherry told me. 'In my twenties, I'd be thinking, "do they like me?" and now I'm like, "hey buddy, what have you got? What do you bring?" The beauty of sex when you're a bit older is to really enjoy it without the insecurities you have when you're younger, which allows you to have a deeper connection.' Amen to that.

*

I am pleased to report that I'm happy being single. I've discovered parts of myself I didn't know existed, and I'm looking forward to exploring more about who I really am – sexually, and otherwise. I don't want to rush into another serious relationship any time soon, because I think I need this time on my own to do a lot of healing. I've learned that I have an unfathomable yearning to be loved, and that I've felt, deep down, that I am unworthy of love. I know this partly came from having emotionally unavailable parents who weren't able to accommodate my needs because they had so much shit going on with themselves, meaning I often felt invisible and unloved. Although the adult me now knows that isn't true, the wounds of the child are hard to shake.

Since my separation, the connections I have had with people have shown me how the same patterns can repeat themselves. My need for unconditional love, which has existed since I was a kid, would still lead to a propensity for co-dependency and losing myself in a relationship. I would become more willing to please them over my own needs, and I needed their love and adoration to validate me. However, now I can see the signs and I have more aware-ness than I previously did to not fall into that hole any more. I have been taking my friends' advice, and nurturing the relationship I have with myself before I am able to have a whole, fulfilling, healthy relationship with someone else. For now, I'm content with prioritising my healing and self-pleasure, and if the opportunity for a casual encounter comes along, where I feel safe and think I could enjoy myself, then I will try not to run and hide. I want to follow what feels right for me, and not just dive into something – romantically and sexually – because I think it would look good or seem good, or because I think it might heal me. And the next time I go on a date, instead of feeling worried about them liking me, I'm going to ask myself 'but more importantly, do you like them?'

Although I'm learning not to channel all my reliance into one person, I'm constantly reminded of how humans aren't built to be lonely, isolated creatures. We crave community and social contact. My separation has taught me to trust my friends and family more, to be open about when I need help and support, and to allow love to seep into my life from different directions. I don't need someone else to make me whole, but I also can't be whole all by myself. We learn so much about ourselves through our interactions with others. Being fiercely independent also means overstretching yourself. Admitting that I do need and want connection and intimacy – even if it doesn't involve sex and romance – has been more wonderful than I could have imagined.

If you're at the starting block of single life, or you're still not sure whether to pull the trigger on your current relationship, I want you to know: I can really relate. Starting afresh is fucking scary. The idea of someone else seeing you naked is fucking scary. Even doing some DIY yourself can feel fucking scary. It doesn't matter how empowered you think you are, allow yourself to feel all these feelings. Navigating change is one of the hardest things we have to do. We're creatures of comfort, stability and habit. But change can also be the most beautiful, fulfilling, *necessary* thing we ever do. Life is short, and we deserve to spend as much time as possible feeling happy and free. We deserve to dive into the ocean and enjoy the deep, warm waters. You might have to battle through some sharks to get there – but you will. I'm telling you this as a reminder to myself too.

Getting through a separation is a marathon, not a sprint, so don't pressure yourself to just get over it. Whether it is your decision or not, the transition is tough and disorientating. I'm not sure I'll ever be completely free of the guilt, and the doubt, and I'll probably always miss the security and comfort cushion of that long-term relationship in some form. No relationship is ever 100% good or bad and it's okay to miss people and still not want to be with them. It's okay to reminisce on the good times and feel sad about the moments you shared with them. But if I hadn't ended my relationship, I never would've had relationships with women and uncovered the true depths of my sexuality. I never would've taken so many of the opportunities I've taken; in fact, I doubt this book would be in your hands right now. I've learned that I am independent and capable and I can do anything I set my mind to, with or without a partner. Ultimately, I've never felt more like me – and I know, in the end, despite the pain, it was all worth it.

What I've learned about sex after separation:

- It can take a while to fully embrace sex after a separation or divorce. Give yourself time, and commit to self-exploration first before diving into another sexual relationship too soon.

- Don't let anyone force you into downloading dating apps before you're ready. They'll still be there as soon as you feel in the right emotional and physical state to date again. Never rush into anything. Everyone moves at their own pace.

- Be clear about your boundaries before any sexual encounter. Most of the time, they will appreciate your honesty and guidance. And if they don't, they're probably not someone you want to have sex with anyway.

- Trust your instincts. If someone makes you feel uncomfortable, or a situation doesn't feel right, it probably isn't. You don't need to follow through with something just to prove that you're moving on.

- It can be hard starting afresh when you're surrounded by people in relationships. Seek out newly divorced or single friends who you can bond with and share your experiences.

- We over-glorify relationships and stigmatise single life, but being single offers you so many opportunities: the chance to experiment, and to discover new experiences. Switch your mindset and embrace everything singledom has to offer.

11

Liberation

So, there I was, lying on that floor in the north London room, with the stranger's finger inside my vagina. I'm 40 years old, freshly divorced, and right in the middle of a 'sacred yoni healing'. It's a sensual tantric practice that involves massaging the 'yoni' (effectively the Sanskrit word for 'pussy') with the purpose of igniting divine feminine energy and, in doing so, enhancing self-confidence, resilience, creativity and pleasure.

I know, I know. It sounds like the kind of woo-woo endeavour that belongs in a Los Angeles reality TV show. I hear you – I would've thought exactly the same thing a few years ago. But, as I've begun to unpack the shame around my body, masturbation and more, I have also been on a much wider quest of self-discovery, which has led me to become increasingly open-minded about all things spiritual and mystical. As I've been questioning so many of my deeply held beliefs, I've thought: how do we actually know what's real and logical, and what isn't? Who gets to decide what is silly and frivolous? What if there is some truth to these (often, ancient) practices? I now look at the planets and read about how they affect the world, and me, using my birth chart. Whether it is 100% true or not, what harm does it do by believing in it? I don't make decisions based on any of this stuff but it adds an extra layer of magic to my life. I smudge sage throughout my house to dispel and guard off negative energy. I use Palo Santo to bring in positivity. I'm addicted to learning about and gathering crystals. I have reiki regularly and have had some pretty sensational experiences. I use meditation to heal my heart and I've had some incredibly transformational moments, where I have broken down and cried. I would strongly recommend that you find your version of spirituality. Whatever it is, find the beauty in just being; find something that helps you tune into the universe. In doing so, I have been led towards some seemingly bonkers activities. And it turns out, they have actually had a massive impact on me, and helped me inch ever closer to sexual freedom. So just hear me out, okay?

I found out about the yoni healing after attending a fascinating workshop about conscious communication, which was all about our ability to clearly and compassionately communicate your truth without blaming, criticising, shaming, projecting and assuming. I learned so much that day. The hosts of the workshop talked us through a model of conscious communication developed by Marshall B. Rosenberg that I have been using ever since when trying to communicate my feelings and boundaries. First, you explain what you observed: what did you see, hear or imagine that didn't contribute to your well-being? Next, say how that made you feel (angry, sad, scared), before requesting what you need (for example, I need to feel heard or valued). Lastly, directly ask a clear and concise request, like, 'I would like you to make sure that, next time, you put your phone away before we go to bed.' It is hugely helpful – it means you're not constantly bringing up all your dirty laundry when you're having a disagreement with a partner (or friend or relative) and they have a clear understanding of how their actions make you feel, and what actions they can do to alleviate that feeling. Genius!

Anyway, one of the hosts was an amazing woman called Amelia – she was wise and warm and I found her energy incredibly soothing and considerate. She felt approachable and welcoming. When I got home, I found her Instagram account, called @alchemywithamelia, and started to flick through her posts. Scrolling down her feed, I saw a post where she said she offered sacred yoni healing, and briefly explained what it was. Flicking through the slides, I discovered that yoni healing can be beneficial if you have experienced sexual trauma, if you've been in a toxic relationship, if you struggle to orgasm or feel disconnected from your feminine essence. It said that yoni healing can help with shame, guilt, judgement and fear around your sexuality and sexual history.

Immediately, I was taken in. I wanted – no, *needed* – to know what it felt like. Not too long ago, I wouldn't have been in the position to hear about something like this, let alone seek it out and experience it. Firstly, I wouldn't have understood the point, and secondly, I'd be far too afraid to allow a stranger to feel the most vulnerable part of my body in such an exposed way. Have a random woman put their finger up my vagina, in the hope of some magical trans-formation? I probably would've laughed. But there I was, getting in touch with Amelia, and booking my session. And as soon as I stepped inside that room to begin the three-hour process, I knew I had made the right decision.

The session began with a tantra heart exercise. This is where you place your hand on the other person's chest, by their heart, and breathe together while looking into each other's eyes without saying a word. The aim is to help you connect with one another, slow down the breath and release oxytocin (the hormone that promotes bonding). After this step, I felt completely calm and trusting. So, it didn't feel strange at all when she asked me to strip naked to begin the 'goddess ceremony', where I stood in the middle of the floor – cellulite, nipples and labia on full display – while she chanted positive affirmations at me. Standing there, I realised just how far I'd come. For so long, I had hated my body, contorting it and hiding it so that people couldn't see it in its full-frontal glory. I used to be disgusted with myself. But in that room, I stood there with pride and knew I had nothing to be ashamed of.

I suddenly understood just how much I had suppressed my desires, my strength, my voice and my courage because I didn't want people to dislike me or to judge me. I had quietened myself because I felt no one was listening, and if they did listen, I was scared they wouldn't accept me. I had made myself as small as I could possibly be so as not to draw attention to myself. Us women are great at that, aren't we? We become the 'good girls' we are told to be – classy, quiet, timid, respectful – and we lose all the rage, all the power that is already there, deep within us. I hoped this yoni healing might help me to remember who the fuck I am. I wanted to find my bold, fearless and sexy side, that was free from all the shame I had attached to it over the years.

When Amelia finally put her finger inside me for the main part of the healing, I could barely feel it. It definitely wasn't the intrusion I expected it to be. In fact, rather than feeling full of power and rage, I felt so peaceful that I drifted off to sleep. But maybe, I realised afterwards, feeling a sense of peace is essential for finding our power. We need to feel at peace in our own skin. We need to feel at peace with our bodies; we need to accept all that they have been through and forgive ourselves – and others. We need to find peace with our desires and with what gives us pleasure. We need to feel completely at peace with our humanity. Perhaps, I thought, shedding shame isn't just about being loud, proud and open. It's also about embracing the quiet. It's about accepting ourselves, and loving ourselves deeply, even when there's no one else in the room.

This wasn't the only spiritual experience I had that led to a revelation. A couple of months later, I attended another workshop, part of which involved a kundalini yoga class. In kundalini yoga, you are guided through different breathing techniques while assuming certain positions or doing particular movements. The idea is to push energy through the spine and open up the chakras to achieve a kind of spiritual awakening. It sounded like exactly my cup of tea, except it was a total battle to get through. I really struggled to stay in it and wanted to get up and walk out so many times during the session. I kept telling myself, 'just surrender, Nat, just surrender' and I managed to push through to the end. And shortly afterwards, I think I did have that spiritual awakening.

At the end of the exercises, I was fucking relieved when the teacher told us to lie back on the yoga mat as she begun a sound bath. Now this I could get behind. If you've never been to a sound bath, I really recommend it. Whether you believe in spirituality or not, it's an incredible experience – you lie there while a teacher uses healing instruments such as gongs, singing bowls, rattles, and other soul-rousing, meditative but extremely powerful sounds. As I lay there feeling the vibrations from the sounds, my whole body started shaking uncontrollably. Now, you'll have to forgive me as I explain this to you. It sounds like unbelievable, mumbo-jumbo shit, but it felt very real to me. My eyes were closed, and I felt the presence of huge shadows in the periphery of the darkness. As I tried to work out what the shadow was, it started to come into view: it appeared to have a face with large, sharp teeth. I know what you're thinking – terrifying, right? Except, weirdly it wasn't. In the background, I could hear the teacher talking about sinking into the ground and letting the earth wrap around and hold you, so I think this is why I felt so safe and protected in the face of this menacing vision I was having.

Suddenly, as the shadow came over me, I noticed that my mind's eye was back on that beach, aged four, where the most traumatic thing happened. I was staring up at a cloudless, bright sky, edged by leaves shaking in a gentle breeze. I was shivering, I must have been cold or shaking from shock that day. Something extraordinary was happening but I didn't know what. Tears were streaming down my face and I had to get out of that room quickly. I didn't want to be there when the other people opened their eyes. I got up quietly, nodded my head towards the door and mouthed, 'can I go?'. The lady leading the session didn't look shocked or surprised and simply nodded back. I went straight home to my bedroom, closed the door and curled up in the foetal position under my duvet, convulsing and rocking gently. I continued crying for the next couple of hours.

I had never experienced anything like this before. As the tears rolled down my face and onto my pillow, it felt like all that shame I had been accumulating my entire life – from my mum's rape on the beach, to my first relationship aged 13, through all the bending, and twisting, and attempting to fit myself into society's expectations – had come to the surface. I felt a shift like I was finally ready to leave all of that behind me, once and for all. I knew that I had come such a long way. I had come through dark, terrifying shadows, and I had made my way into serene sunlight. It felt like that session was a culmination of everything that came before, and it made me realise just how much I had transformed. Shame, I understood, would no longer define me. I think this is what you might call a 'breakthrough'. Once my tears had dried, I felt like I had been reborn. And I want that kind of breakthrough for you, too.

*

Liberation

Look, I know that kind of spiritual stuff isn't for everyone. But there are so many different ways you can go on your own journey of discovery, to get to the real 'you' and leave all the shame you've been harbouring behind you. One really simple way of doing that, which really helped me, is reading and listening. I got super into self-help and non-fiction books around the time I started my blog, when I was pregnant with my second daughter. I thought it was just a hobby, but I realise now that I was looking for answers to questions I didn't even know I had. I wanted to understand more about the world around me, and myself. I read *Why I'm No Longer Talking to White People About Race* by Reni Eddo-Lodge, and I learned about how racism had – consciously and unconsciously – shaped me. I read *The Beauty Myth* by Naomi Wolf and I started to understand how society's obsession with women's bodies had seeped into my whole being. Over the years, I expanded my mind by reading inspiring calls-to-action like *Daring Greatly* by Brené Brown, *Big Magic* by Elizabeth Gilbert, *The Power of Now* by Eckhart Tolle and *What I Know For Sure* by Oprah Winfrey, and I started to realise that there was a bigger world out there for me, and I wasn't selfish for wanting to grab it by the horns. All of these books planted new seeds in my mind and allowed me to escape and dream of all the possibilities I hadn't dared let in. I was evolving, and the little box room in my head was bulging open.

In 2020, I read Glennon Doyle's memoir, *Untamed*, about breaking free from the shackles of misogyny and finding love with a woman, and it resonated with me incredibly deeply. It reflected my life in so many ways. Days before I finally ended my marriage, I read her detailing her indecision about ending her own relationship and looking for answers in every corner, even googling whether she should stay with her husband. She knew the answer already, like I did, but we both allowed the indecision to eat us up inside. I know that it gave me the push I needed. I'm sure Glennon's story wouldn't resonate with everyone, and I'm sure mine won't either. But when you do find yourself in someone else's story, even in a small way, it's a uniquely powerful way of getting to know yourself better. Reading and listening to the stories of others, and finding myself reflected in them, gave me the distinct sensation that my thoughts are valid. That my feelings are felt by so many other people. That it's not self-absorbed to feel a lot, and to want a lot.

Of course, I can't talk about self-understanding without addressing how amazing therapy is. Though, it has to be acknowledged that the financial cost of seeing a therapist is a huge privilege. Although some forms of therapy are available on the NHS (usually with very long waiting lists), and some places offer means-tested therapy, where you pay proportionally to your earnings, it's usually a massive economic undertaking. I started officially going to individual therapy once my marriage ended and, at any other time in my life, I wouldn't have been in a position to do so. I'm so grateful that I was able to, though, because it helped me to unravel so many of my deeply held beliefs.

The only way you can get the most out of therapy is by being completely honest. There's a strong temptation to hold back and not talk about all of your deepest secrets, especially the ones surrounded by shame. You have to build so much trust, and then be willing to uncover the whole truth. I would make the same mistakes time and again, and I'd feel embarrassed admitting them to my therapist. But their job is not to judge – it's to help you unlock your true self and give you awareness as to why you make certain decisions, and suggest tools to help you make better ones.

I'm not sure writing this book would have been possible had I not gone to therapy. It has equipped me with the tools and understanding to dig deeper. It has given me a stronger sense of self. In fact, it was my therapist who first pointed out that I might have Attention Deficit Hyperactivity Disorder, also known as ADHD, which eventually led to my diagnosis and hugely enhanced my understanding of my own behaviours. I wasn't useless and incapable, like I'd always believed. I'm now on medication, which has made a massive difference to my productivity and focus. Therapy can mean different things to different people, but when I spoke to Professor Tanya Byron about this, a clinical psychologist who practices as a therapist, broadcasts on the BBC and has a weekly mental health column in *The Times*, she said that therapy can often be 'to help people make order out of chaos. It gives people another perspective. Someone might be looking out of one window at the view of their life and a therapist offers another view and suggests, "let's look out of this one instead".'

You might worry that digging into your issues in therapy will reveal unsightly and upsetting truths that you won't be able to handle, but psychotherapist Charlotte Fox Weber had a reassuring answer for this: 'What's astonishing is that we can deal with whatever is there – however painful. What we run away from tends to haunt us and get in our way. Therapy is essentially about emotional freedom, and it's liberating and expansive to discover the layers of our existence.'

If therapy isn't an option for you, there are tons of books written by therapists and experts that can really enhance your relationship with yourself. There's *Find Your True Voice* by Emmy Brunner, who guides us through the process of recovery and manifesting a life worth living. The book *Attached*, by Amir Levine and Rachel S. F. Heller, can point you towards your attachment style – you can find out whether you are anxious, secure or avoidant, and how that manifests in your relationships, in order to make changes. A personal favourite of mine is also *The 5 Love Languages* by Dr Gary Chapman, where you can learn which of the love languages are most important to you – words of affirmation, receiving gifts, acts of service, quality time, physical touch – and therefore learn how to communicate them with your partner. And *How to Do the Work* by Dr Nicole LePera had a monumental effect on me. There are also some incredible psychotherapy podcasts, like Esther Perel's 'Where Should We Begin?', which follows real-life couples' counselling sessions, and Tanya Byron's own podcast called 'How Did We Get Here?', which she hosts alongside Claudia Winkleman, giving insight into therapeutic conversations.

In doing all these things, I started to rediscover my inner voice; a voice I realised I had lost somewhere along the way. Only recently, I remembered that when I was a teenager, I used to question myself frequently about whether I was happy. It was a very conscious decision, almost like I was directly communicating with a deeper, fuller version of myself. I'd be lying on my bed, and I would say to myself, clearly: 'Nat, are you happy?' Most of the time, the answer was 'yes'. And if it wasn't, then I knew I needed to change something. But it wasn't just about specific events – I constantly questioned my life choices and my relationships. 'Nat, are you happy?' When the answer was 'no', I knew something had to shift. When the answer was 'yes', I felt comfortable and secure in the life I was leading.

The relationship you have with your inner voice is the most important one you have. I believe there's an all-knowing version of yourself deep inside your soul, that knows when you're in danger, when you're unsafe, what you desire and what you need, before your conscious self has even worked it out. And the more you can listen to that voice, the more you'll be able to find the life you're destined to lead. In *Untamed*, Glennon Doyle described this little voice as your 'Knowing', which I think is a great name for it, but I guess you could simply call it a gut feeling. The problem is, we often ignore that voice; the part of our soul that knows who we truly are and what we truly want. We muffle it with gender roles, society's expectations, what we think we should do, and what we think we should want. We have to make a very conscious effort to tune in and listen to it, to have an active conversation with it, otherwise our sense of self starts to drift away.

Now, I'm in a constant dialogue with myself. I make time to check in and it's easy for you to do the same. Make time appointments with yourself. You don't have to do anything fancy – but schedule time into your calendar to just check in – but you do need to be very conscious about it at first. Treat yourself like a good friend or relative – someone you'd be happy to commit time and energy to listening to. You might think rushing around, looking after everyone and working crazy hours, is a badge of honour. But, trust me, you will not get a 'good girl' certificate at the end of your life for working yourself to the bone, neglecting yourself and only focusing on others. I'm not talking about abandoning all your responsibilities and running off to retreats every other week (although wouldn't that be lovely?) – I'm just talking 15 minutes in your day, to schedule time where you don't look at your phone, and no one is allowed to demand you give them some biscuits or find the worm tablets for an itchy bum. Spend that time just breathing. You don't have to meditate, you don't have to do any fancy breath work – just sit or lie and be. You have no idea how beneficial this is until you do it. It gives you time to process, to think, to listen to your inner voice, to steer your own bus instead of just reacting.

Funnily enough, spending more time with myself has helped me improve my closest relationships, and leave behind the ones that aren't working any more. When it comes to friends, I will ask myself: do I have a good time when I'm around them? Do I look forward to seeing them? If the answer is anything but 'yes', I ask: what needs to change? Should I start distancing myself from them? Is it me that needs to change my expectations of this person, or maybe they need to change theirs of me. Your connections – whether romantic or platonic – aren't always going to be sunshine and light, but there's a tipping point and that limit will be different for everyone. Questioning yourself regularly keeps you focused on who, and what, makes your life great.

We learn about the self through our interactions with others. Analyse the connections you have in your life – you will learn everything you need to know about how you view your self-worth through the relationship dynamics you have with others. Do you allow people to walk all over you, to constantly break your boundaries, or do they listen when you speak, care for you and attend to your needs? I'm not saying it's your fault if people are horrible to you, but simply that those interactions are the window to your soul. And look at yourself too: do you try to control or guilt-trip or blame? Are you the pinnacle of passive-aggression? The power of listening to how others perceive you is illuminating. And remember: I said perceive, not judge. Self-reflection is an incredible tool to utilise.

Journaling has also been game-changing. When it was first suggested to me, I thought: 'I already think it, why do I have to write it down too? Isn't that just adding to my workload?' Well, yes, it requires some extra work but what you get in return is bountiful. Sometimes, I wake up and just sit down and vomit all my meandering thoughts and concerns onto the page. It helps clear my mind when it feels over-crowded and foggy. When I read it back, I'm able to rationalise my illogical thoughts. Sometimes, I use prompts. You can find tons of journal prompts online, but ones I like to use are: How are you feeling? What are your happiest memories? When did you last feel at peace/powerful/balanced? What is stressing you out? What changes need to be made in your life? If you weren't scared, what would you do tomorrow? By doing this, I'm able to clarify my wants and desires; I can create gratitude and enhance my self-worth. It's such an easy task, but it's so powerful. In fact, writing things down has scientific backing – one study found that people who wrote for 20 minutes a day, for four days in a row, had a marked mood improvement.

Another big way I connect to myself is through dancing. I found dance classes a few years ago, which I love. It is a brilliant form of meditation for me because I have to concentrate really hard on following the choreography, therefore I am unable to think about anything else during the one-hour class. It's also helped me connect with my body again and explore being silly, being sexy, or being powerful through movement. I even dance naked in the rain now! The feeling of freedom is incredible. One day, when I was alone in the house, I had just come out of the shower in my towel when I noticed it was raining outside. For some reason, it just looked so appealing to me. I wanted to feel the rain on my skin (*à la* Natasha Bedingfield) so I dropped my towel and ran outside. Yes, I live in a goldfish bowl of terraced houses, but it felt like I was truly reconnecting to my natural essence. Now, I do it whenever I fancy, and it feels like the ultimate 'I don't give a fuck' – it's just the definition of liberation when I dance around naked in my back garden. Something about the rain just amplifies that feeling. If you live near water, jump in the sea, and float around looking up at the clouds. I wish I lived near the sea – I'm drawn to water when I feel overwhelmed or in need of emotional support. Water heals, water holds, water washes away. Don't underestimate its power.

Liberation

Nurturing my relationship with myself has, I believe, been the final stop on my journey towards finding sexual freedom. For so long, I had looked for pleasure and validation in all the wrong places. I thought my partners should be able to read my mind, and then felt disappointed when they inevitably couldn't. News flash: if you're not in an open, productive, loving dialogue with yourself, you're never going to be able to have those kinds of conversations with other people. Before, I would've believed that turning inward was inherently selfish – but, actually, it has completely opened me up to other people's perspectives. I've realised that we're all just dealing with our own shit; we all have flaws, fears and we've made mistakes that haunt us. It has made me so much more empathetic to what other people are going through, to what other people's wants and needs are. The trick is to try to understand each other, and then meet somewhere in the middle.

*

As I write this, it feels like I'm entering a new phase in my life. I feel open and hungry to embrace new experiences, and I want to make a difference. Instead of closing myself off to all of my inner strength, I want to pour that energy out into the world.

So, I've made some major changes. I have started doing a counselling course, because I want to support others in the same way that I have been supported. By the end, I will have a counselling diploma. And I've signed up for some sexual healing training, so I can delve further into my own sexual healing and spirituality, before eventually being able to help other people tackle their own. I have also started working on a not-for-profit organisation project that has been whirring around in my head for some time now. After all I have learned in my journey, I want this platform to educate about sex and sensuality differently to what we are used to. I want to provide inclusive, shame-free, judgement-free, anti-discriminatory sex education for adults, while challenging societal rules and norms. The organisation will also aim to change legislation and laws that are unfair and discriminate against women, for example, when it comes to flexible working and victim blaming in rape cases. The aim is that it will be led by a collective of people who adults and kids alike want to hear from – activists, creatives, people who are shape-shifting the current climate; people who are doing work on the ground.

I feel more galvanised than ever to be more vocal about these topics that are important to me. I'm no longer shackled by other people's opinions; I can't be fucked any more with shrinking myself into being an 'acceptable' woman. I'm not letting myself worry about who might look at me disapprovingly. I encourage you to do the same. Even family members and those closest to you might not like or agree with the things you say or do. It's okay – you don't need to have everyone's approval all the time. They are not living your life and they have no right to clip your wings. Allow your spirit to shine bright, proud and loud – and do it with conviction, for fuck's sake. Stop apologising for existing and start to love yourself like your life depends on it.

Liberation

Most importantly: stay curious about going deeper, about learning more, constantly challenging and questioning your thoughts, decisions and behaviours. Commit to healing from past traumas, in the knowledge that it will be brutal but amazingly worthwhile. Learn to sit with difficult emotions – write them out, talk them out. Allow yourself to be vulnerable with people. Being strong, capable and unemotional will only lead to resentment further down the line. Speak your truth, even if that means losing people along the way. But take baby steps, be kind and patient with yourself.

Instead of waiting to be a stone lighter or for your skin to be smoother or for your hair to be longer, do that thing now. Buy the dress, try that new hobby, say 'yes' to doing the thing that scares you the most, make that decision you've been putting off – because we only have the now and you are too important to keep delaying yourself from living because you're worried about how you might be perceived. You deserve to be held, to be treasured, to laugh, to live and to love whoever you want to. You can walk the road less travelled. You are magical and powerful and whatever it was that made you lose your voice or dampen your spirit is worth seeking out and snuffing out (metaphorically speaking, before I get my arse sent to jail for inciting women to strangle their exes). Enjoy your body, embrace your sensuality, make time for connection and wank to your heart's content. View it as making love to yourself. You deserve that much.

My journey through sex has led me here, to this exact moment. I entered the world as a scared little girl, shrouded by shame from the moment I was born, and I grew into a woman who judged, shamed and blamed herself – and other women. I was trapped inside a cage of society's making; a cage that forced me to be a 'good girl', to behave, to have a perfect body and be a perfect mother and wife. I shamed myself for my own thoughts; I felt guilty all the time. I wanted nothing more than to fit in, to embrace the pre-designed mould, and follow the path intended for me. That's no way to live. None of us should settle for that kind of life.

Slowly but surely, I have unravelled all the layers of bull-shit that have been weighing me down. I've learned that my sexuality belongs to me, and me only. I've learned that anything can be 'for' me if I want it to be – whether that's watching porn, or doing DIY. I've learned that relation-ships require real work, and they won't solve all your problems. I've learned that there's no one-size-fits-all for being a good mother. I've learned that heterosexuality isn't the default, and that single life can be just as rewarding and empowering as long-term commitment. I've learned that most of my previously held beliefs were by-products of systems designed to repress and hold women back. We have to fight against them, to return to what makes us truly who we are. We often forget that we are all simply animals. Bold, beautiful, free animals; guided by pleasure and our search for meaning and connection. Sex might seem like a small part of life, but actually I think it's a microcosm for everything. If we feel free in the way we have sex, if we can express ourselves sexually with joy and abandon, then I think the rest will fall into place. If we can be vulnerable enough to let people inside us (physically and metaphorically), then we open ourselves up to all the wonder and awe that life has to offer. Sex is fucking important. It creates life. It's the best natural drug in the world. It's time to bring it out of the darkness and into bright searing light – awkwardness, funny smells, self-consciousness, sweaty thighs and all.

I won't pretend that it's easy to replace shame with freedom. I also won't pretend I have completed that transition. As with everything, there isn't a golden pot at the end of the rainbow, as much as we wish there was. Shame might not be a constant companion any more, but it still creeps up on me every once in a while, like when I find myself comparing my body to other women on Instagram, or when my kids act out and I worry I'm a shit mother. But I know I'm doing the best I can. Now I have greater clarity, like a camera lens fogged up with steam has finally cleared.

Here's what I know now: Wanting and needing sex is valid. Your pleasure is important. You are not bad or dirty for being sexy and sexual, even if you've birthed humans. Your sexual history is not a moral compass – you can be a good, kind human and still love sex. The awful things that happened to you weren't your fault. You are beautiful, not despite but *because of* your flaws. As long as it's safe, consensual and brings you joy, you can love whoever you want to love. You can be whoever you want to be. More than anything, your sexual power is divine and it's only right and fair that you nurture it every day. As hard as it can be to let go of, shame has no place in your heart or your soul. It doesn't belong there. I know that by learning to feel myself, I was actually learning to heal myself. And if you're only just starting on that journey now – I salute you. It's about to be one hell of a ride.

Epilogue

I've wanted to write a book for as long as I can remember. I think I wanted to write a book before I understood what writing one actually meant. A desire to have my voice heard and my words in indelible ink. I often get asked why I'm so open and honest about my life and struggles on social media. Sometimes friends and family think it's weird that I divulge so much. I've done many things that I'm not proud of, we all have, but I now understand why I did them and I forgive myself. I also forgive myself for the many things that happened to me that I had no control over. Now I control the narrative of my life, not my past traumas. For me, sharing my truth in all its messy and imperfect beauty has been my way of healing. I no longer feel like I'm carrying around a load of dirty little secrets that someone will one day expose and threaten me with. It's all out there, for you to see. No one can shame me, for I've already shared and released them.

Since I left my marriage, writing this book and the process of looking inwards has been incredibly illuminating. The light has shown up the good and the bad, the beautiful and the ugly sides of who I am – often parts I have tried to run away from and bury a long time ago. As you'll know by now, there is no escaping. The book also forced me to have some very difficult conversations. The result was a deeper understanding and connection with myself and the people I love. My healing is far from complete and new curveballs come in all the time that sweep me off my feet. Today though, I feel strong enough to challenge the long-held beliefs and negative patterns.

I will and you will never be perfect; we will fuck up. But it's about accepting that mistakes happen and giving ourselves grace – striving to understand ourselves better, be more patient and loving to ourselves, and letting the waves of forgiveness wash over us time and time again. Forgiveness is a fundamental part of the healing process. Words that would have probably repelled me before – awareness, acceptance, learning, forgiveness, growth and healing – I now hold dear to my soul. As if you go through life being reborn with each new rise of the sun, allow yourself to evolve, adapt, travel and adjust. One day you will realise you are strong enough to take back control of your story. We have so many magical moments yet to come, especially when we are holding the baton and conducting our own orchestra.

Nat x

Book List

Attached by Amir Levine and Rachel S. F. Heller

The Beauty Myth by Naomi Wolf

Becoming Cliterate by Dr Laurie Mintz

Big Magic by Elizabeth Gilbert

Come as You Are by Emily Nagoski

Daring Greatly by Brené Brown

Eight Dates by John Gottman and Julie Schwartz Gottman

Find Your True Voice by Emmy Brunner

Get Divorced, Be Happy by Helen Thorn

Hard Core by Linda Williams

How to Do the Work by Dr Nicole LePera

How to Heal a Broken Heart by Rosie Green

Mind The Gap by Dr Karen Gurney

Pornland: How Porn Has Hijacked Our Sexuality by Gail Dines

Feeling Myself

The Power of Now by Eckhart Tolle

The Purity Myth by Jessica Valenti

A Radical Awakening by Dr Shefali Tsabary

Sex Ed by Ruby Rare

The Sex Issue (compiled by Goop, featuring Esther Perel)

Untamed by Glennon Doyle

Virgin: The Untouched History by Hanne Blank

What I Know For Sure by Oprah Winfrey

Why I'm No Longer Talking to White People About Race by Reni Eddo-Lodge

What We Want by Charlotte Fox Weber

The 5 Love Languages by Dr Gary Chapman

Acknowledgements

Firstly, I would like to say thank you, Sam, and the team at Penguin Random House for giving me this opportunity. Thank you to Arielle for being patient and understanding during the particularly laborious and traumatising writing/ editing process. We became sisters for a moment in time, who bickered and battled because we were so intertwined in each other's lives. Your skills, input and the way you pulled it all together are the makings of this book. To my mum, the first time I sent you a chapter I thought I was going to be sick. I knew how desperately hard this book would be for you; thank you for giving me your blessing. Thank you for battling your demons, setting aside your own needs and giving me my voice back. You are the epitome of a warrior. No one should ever have to go through the things you have. One day I hope to support you to tell your whole story if you want to, because boy is there more! Mum, it was never your fault. You are my hero; my one true everlasting love and I will always be by your side. My longed-for sisters, I am your biggest fan and I will always be in your corner. To my daughters, my biggest teachers, I will forever try to do better because of you. To my therapist who helped me turn my life around when I was on the floor.

Feeling Myself

Hunting you down because I'd seen you on telly and knew your direct, no-bullshit style was exactly what I needed was the best investment in myself I've ever made. To the first woman I loved (romantically), we gave each other the highest highs, the lowest lows and the deepest, most trans-formational lessons in life and understanding ourselves – I will never not love you. To all the women I have loved, love and will love – you have my heart in your hands. Your love, guidance and support mean everything to me. To all the women who have endured unimaginable things, you are not broken or damaged. I love you.

Nat x

Index

Index